MOTHER SUN

a journaled memoir

HAYLEY PEARLMAN

illustrated by
samira huke

the legend of the dandelion:
adapted from Carolyn Sherwin Bailey

Once long, long ago, the Angel of the flowers came down to Earth. She wandered here and there, in field, and forest, and garden, to find the flower she loved the most. As she hurried on her search, she came upon a tulip, all orange and red, standing stiff and proud in a garden, and the Angel said to the tulip: "Where should you like most of all to live?"

"I should like to live on a castle lawn in the velvety grass," said the tulip, "where my colors would show against the gray castle walls. I should like to have the princess tell me how beautiful I am."

But the Angel turned away with sad eyes from the proud tulip, and spoke to the rose.

"Where should you like most to stay?" she asked the rose.

"I should like to climb the castle walls," said the rose, "for I am fragile, and delicate, and not able to climb myself. I need help and shelter."

The Angel of the flowers turned sadly away from the rose, and hurried on until she came to the sturdy, yellow dandelion growing in the meadow grass.

"And where should you like most of all to live?" asked the Angel to the dandelion.

"Oh," cried the dandelion, "I want to live wherever the happy children may find me when they run by to school, or play in the fields. I want to live by the roadside, and in the meadows, and push between the stones in the city yards and make everyone happy because of my bright colors...."

"You are the flower I love the most," said the Angel, as she laid her hand upon the dandelion's curly, yellow head. "You shall blossom everywhere from spring till fall, and be the children's flower."

That is why the dandelion comes so early and pushes her head up everywhere—by hedge, and field, and hut, and wall...and why she has such a long, sweet life.

Fathers be good to your daughters
Daughters will love like you do
Girls become lovers who turn into mothers
So mothers be good to your daughters, too.

- John Mayer

My mother was once my family's sun; the directional pull we
followed in a familiar warm orbit. And when our sun passed onward
from this life, all members were individually lost and spun off
center. It wasn't until seven years later, when I gave birth to my
son, that I made a commitment to understand where my beautiful
mother had gone when she died.

And so, *Mother Sun* began.

The years of motherhood recorded in this journal, have gently
forced me to learn how to grow like that dandelion flower:

I am not a tulip. I am not the proud rose. And I'm not a famous
blogger or social media personnel who landed a book deal.

I am a simple dandelion. I am a young mother who believed in her
ability to create her own reality—to grow wherever, and however
she wanted, under the guiding light of her mothering sun.

This is the story of *how* I grew.

And how you, too, can grow—if you simply learn to let the light in.

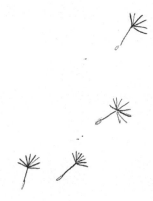

PART ONE
12 ENTRIES

APRIL 4, 2016

two days

Simple and fresh and fair from winter's close emerging...
Forth from its sunny nook of shelter'd grass—innocent,
golden, calm as the dawn,
The spring's first dandelion shows its trustful face.

-Walt Whitman

Everett Jay Pearlman. Born April 2, 12:40 a.m. Weighed 8.56 ounces, 20.5 inches long.

I have never been so in love with anyone or so unaware of myself. It's like I'm changing every minute, molding into my baby's mother: sometimes that feels terrifying, and other times, I feel as if I have finally arrived to where I've always wanted to be, home with a husband and baby.

I was just soaking in the bath, my tub filled with dried herbs that are supposed to heal my sore and aching body, and I kept crying as the warm flowing water covered and comforted what feels like the post-birth blues.

Cradling my cheeks in the support of my hands, I hung my head limped and somewhat lifeless, wondering why you aren't here to meet Everett...why you cannot witness me as a newly born mother.

Where will I tell him you've gone? How will I explain why you are not here? Because I myself can't even answer those tormenting questions.

This should be the most thrilling time of my life. And yet, I haven't missed you this much since the initial loss.

But I can already feel my baby's love starting to heal my still broken pieces. Every space in my body and mind is continually filling with the thought and smell and feeling of my child. Life prior to him already feels impossible trying to imagine, like there's a permanently marked "before" and "after" Everett rift in my years, and suddenly, I know nothing about my person will ever be the same.

I've already taken too much time to write—Everett is sleeping downstairs in Nana's arms and I want to rest while I have the opportunity. I just felt like I needed to talk, even if writing to you in a journal is somewhat make-believe.

I'm so glad he's a boy. (And all that time I was so convinced of a girl.)

He is perfect—absolutely perfect.

APRIL 10, 2016

hiraeth: (n.) a homesickness for a home to which you cannot return, a home which maybe never was: the nostalgia, the yearning, the grief for the lost pieces of your past.

-Merriam Webster Dictionary

I can't really explain how I've missed you recently, but I do know that I've simply been too tired and too occupied, to really realize and fully comprehend your obvious absence.

It's your birthday today. I keep thinking what fun it would be to have a big party for you, or how I'd love returning to the comfort of my childhood home, with you still there to greet me in the familiar kitchen filled with family. Or what it would be like watching you blow out a numbered "47" birthday candle, cradling your new grandson in your arms, while welcoming another year around the sun.

Everett has innocently swallowed up every corner of my brain, but with what little remaining space I own, the pain I'm experiencing with breastfeeding is a constant thought I cannot escape.

Just a few days ago, at his first newborn appointment, the pediatrician assured me that my nursing pain was normal, even offering to watch Everett latch in the hopes of consoling my complaints. I was willing to accept assurance from anyone, so I pulled my sore breast out of my bra and immediately, milk dribbled out in an orderly drip. This elder male pediatrician, dressed in a brown-themed tweed suit with matching loafers that looked like a pair Fodder would wear, said, "Well it certainly seems like you have good supply."

It was humiliating.

And Chris was standing there, observing it all, too shy and out of place to say anything or even slightly laugh to diffuse my embarrassment.

But the doctor said everything looked great with our feeding and that I just needed to give it some time. I left the office feeling confidently happy, silently promising myself to quit doubting my abilities and just own this whole nursing experience.

After two more twingeful days passed, I finally trusted something wasn't right. So I called a lactation consultant at The Midwife Center, who told me to come in and see her right away—that the excessive discomfort was not normal.

I was scheduled a last-minute appointment for that afternoon, but still couldn't drive myself there. It had only been six days since giving birth, and I felt scared to use the car seat and drive with Everett. I had never done it before.

Chris was working from home but couldn't leave his computer. Grandma happened to be sick and Nana was somewhere. I felt helpless and out of options, angry that the dependence of you was no longer dependable. You'd think after so many years, I would've understood and accepted this by now, but something about having Everett has broken apart my common sense and replaced it all with hormonal emotion.

I ended up calling Aunt Sara, and she put her whole day on hold to help me out. I was thankful and relieved.

When she and I got back into the lactation consultant's cozy little office, I was stationed in an egg-shaped chair with pillows stuffed under my arms, and nursed Everett in different positions. The latch felt a little better, but that's because he was literally professionally positioned onto me, and I was fueled with an irrational sense of optimism and determination.

It didn't take long for the consultant to confidently confirm he had tongue-tie. She explained that the thick tissue under his tongue, was tethered down too tightly to the bottom of his mouth. So unable to properly lift his tongue, this was most likely the cause of my excessive discomfort while feeding.

We'd been denied a proper latch for an entire week.

I want to breastfeed Everett, and it seems the only way for me to do that, is to schedule an appointment at Children's Hospital, where they'll do a quick procedure, snipping the tissue and essentially freeing his tongue.

I feel selfish for choosing to put my baby through that, even if it's only for a few seconds. But I don't want to use formula, and right now, I think this is the best choice for the both of us.

Our appointment is in one week, so in the meantime, I'm going to pump my milk and bottle feed—wish me luck.

APRIL 28, 2016

If you're feeling frightened about what comes next, don't be. Embrace the uncertainty. Allow it to lead you places. Be brave as it challenges you to exercise both your heart and your mind as you create your own path toward happiness. And if you should ever look up and find yourself lost, simply take a breath and start over. Retrace your steps and go back to the purest place in your heart...where your hope lives. You'll find your way again.

-Everwood

The other night, Dad and Terri visited and brought Girasole takeout. It felt good to be comforted by the food you and I and our family used to enjoy, at our most coveted restaurant.

After eating my portion of gnocchi, I sat in the corner of the couch and nursed Everett, my toes having cringed and curled when he latched. His tongue-tie appointment was a week ago, so I don't know if it's too soon to tell, but nothing feels different while feeding, which has left me feeling both guilty and absolutely frustrated—even somewhat ashamed.

I wanted to cry the entire time he nursed. And when I was looking down at Everett, lost in our little moment, I heard Terri's voice and it startled me into the reminding surprise that she was there and you weren't. Tears took over my eyes. A droplet landed of my baby's cheek, and I felt sorry and responsible for your absence from him.

I've been walking around the house topless at all times—nothing, not a thin tank or even the sheets can touch me without stinging pain. Nana has been here a lot helping me, and today when I walked down the stairs with my top hanging down and entire chest exposed, she said, "I feel like I've traveled to Africa again!" We had a good laugh.

She's cleaned my toilet, folded loads of laundry, made lunch, and thrown away my blood-soaked postpartum diapers. I literally do not know what I would do without her now or ever, for that matter; she seems like the last real piece of you I have left, besides for my siblings.

My only alternative to alleviate pain has been to continue pumping. Another consultant from a breastfeeding clinic advised me to pump every two hours, for fifteen minutes, in order to boost my supply. But now I feel like I'm stuck in a cycle of pumping milk, using tubes of lanolin, and worrying with each session, just how many ounces I'm going to make. And then shortly after, feeding Everett a bottle, only to start the entire process over in another hour or so.

I've also developed mastitis, because apparently the pump doesn't empty out your milk as entirely or efficiently as a baby, so I got clogged ducts, became sore and engorged, with red spider-like splotches overtaking my breasts. I didn't even know mastitis was something to watch out for.

Simply put, I'm overwhelmed.

There seems to be this immense pressure to breastfeed. On social media, there are women who artfully pose in their bed or bathtub, capturing beautiful pictures of them nursing their babies and toddlers. These moms look stunning and intimate and the whole breastfeeding thing looks so absolutely natural, like it comes easy and without effort.

Throughout my pregnancy, I followed these motherly-like accounts, pickling my brain in a kind of brine that saw these images as normal. *My baby and I will look like this while nursing.*

Even the organic cotton clothes and designer bassinets and nurseries decorated with natural eucalyptus plants, are far from what my life actually looks like. And I like to think of myself as a "hip" person with a grounded sense of taste and style—but I don't have unlimited amounts of money to purchase these baby luxuries, nor do I have thousands and thousands of online followers to show them off for.

The expensive bassinet I saw on Instagram and therefore had to buy, turned out to be completely impractical on our very first night home. Everett preferred the Fisher Price "Rock n' Play" that I once rolled my eyes at, not able to get over its cheapness and cheesy colors. But he loves the way it holds and supports him, and sleeps so very soundly at night as it continually rocks.

But honestly, why am I having so much difficulty nursing? What am I missing? How many more consultants should I see or how many more books do I have to read?

Part of me wants to ignore the cultural norm and say, *Screw it— formula it is!* The other part wants to keep pushing forward, because all my life, that is how I've handled situations. But ultimately, I don't picture us breastfeeding, a knowing-feeling that's slowly pulsing itself present.

Prior to having him, I never even considered not nursing as an option, but I've also been wrong about absolutely everything (his due date, gender, birth, recovery, etc.). But I'm learning.

When it comes to being Everett's mother, my gut is my strongest guide. Even if the midwives or all the blogs and books I read, say that breastfeeding is the best, I am starting to feel that for my son and I, it's not. I mean, nutritionally speaking, of course it's the preferred option—but I feel like I can no longer force this process anymore. I'm ready to stop comparing his mouth and my nipples as two sworn enemies. I'm ready to simply start enjoying Everett and make the final decision to stop nursing and even pumping.

And while I cannot explain the amount of relief I already feel within just writing that, it's hard not to feel like I'm failing my son.

I just need to stop doubting myself and my personal verdicts. That has been a tough ideal to grasp and put into practice. I am truly the only one who can make decisions for myself as a mother—not even you could tell me what to do.

Since seventeen years old, I've been becoming me without you, a factor that has shaped me into an even more independent and strong-willed human, capable of making choices without others' input because I had to continue growing up without yours.

I've just never been "becoming a mother" before, and nothing has felt more difficult to do without you.

MAY 1, 2016

one month

I say to my child, I will explain as much of life as I can, but you must remember that there is a part of life for which you are the explanation.

-Robert Brault

To commemorate successfully surviving the first month of motherhood, I'd like to tell you my birth story. I don't want to write it down for the purpose of preserving details, because right now, I feel as if every moment of Everett's delivery has been invisibly inked to my skin. Rather, I need to write to help me heal...to ensure that I don't take that day and bury its scary memory, never allowing a necessary chance for release.

I was asleep until around eleven o'clock in the evening, when I felt my very first contraction. Still thinking the sensation could be the regular cramps I'd been getting, I tried to resume sleep, but less than eight minutes later, another contraction came. And then another. I woke Chris and told him I was pretty sure labor had started.

Since I was eleven days past my due date, all I'd been wanting were contractions. But when I realized they were real and there to stay, I couldn't believe it was the actual start of meeting our baby. So to relax, I took a bath and shortly after, lost my mucus plug, feeling giddy to see a foreign glob in the toilet when I flushed. *This is actually happening!*

Before the sun rose and the next morning officially began, we started to make our drive to The Midwife Center. My contractions were being timed roughly five minutes apart.

We arrived, only to have the staff say we were early. I was still able to hold a conversation, a sign that told them I wasn't into active labor yet. But we decided to stay anyways. Chris and I settled into our room (it was only one of three: The Midwife Center is comprised of a very small row house in the heart of Pittsburgh) and tried to take a short nap together on the full-sized bed I'd later deliver on.

During each contraction, without intentionally trying, I began to visualize you and I together, standing towards one another. You'd gently blow what looked like glitter from the palm of your hand, and I'd breathe in the scattering golden specks. And then when I exhaled, green ivy-like leaves brushed down the sides of my stomach, taking the pain away.

It seems so strange to picture, but somehow I felt like you were guiding my mind onto a straight plane of concentration.

Twelve hours had now passed since labor initially started, but when my cervix was checked, I was still under 4 cm. I was encouraged over and over to take a long walk outside, so finally I obeyed, and once that was completed, I got into the big jacuzzi tub, where my contractions really started to intensify.

The hot water felt incredible. When I'd get really sweaty after a contraction, Chris would pour cool water over my shoulders, and the simple act allowed us to feel like somewhat of a team. For all the hours before, I knew he was there, but part of a constant background I couldn't plant my attention on. He felt helpless, stuck between wanting to give me space, wanting to help, and having no idea what to do.

My doula told me she really thought I was close to 8 cm and I remember thinking, *I can absolutely do this*. Hours had passed, I had walked, I had relaxed in the tub; I was hopeful my next cervix check would reveal significant progress, but I'd only made it 2 cm further.

I circled around that little confined room, cursing and in complete denial of my slow progress. I said I was done, that this was all so stupid and I could not make it to the end. If drugs were available, this is the point where I would have gladly taken them, despite how much I wanted a "natural" birth.

My body felt comprised of jelly, and I knew the hardest part was yet to come—I still had to get this baby *out*. Active labor had really only just started and already, I was exhausted. By this point, it was probably around dinnertime.

Wanting to rest and float without effort, I returned to the jacuzzi, beginning to become loud and audible. Noise seemed to be the only thing that helped.

Chris was again sitting on the side of the tub and I told him, "If I could survive losing my mom, I can do this." I was staring straight ahead at the shower wall tile, with salty water swelling in my eyes.

Your death and Everett's birth, were the two hardest moments in my life thus far.

After yet another chunk of amounted time (at this point I had been in labor for twenty-six hours), I stood up out of the jacuzzi, letting out the loudest scream yet. I could then hear the nurses and midwife come rushing down the narrow hall towards my room. They wanted me on the bed, and I fought them, wanting to deliver right where I was.

I felt so much pressure inside my groin, like a watermelon wanted through my body. And it didn't just feel like a wide watermelon, but a very heavy one, too. For the first time I actually felt scared, because I had absolutely no idea how this melon was going to safely escape my body.

Within seconds of crawling onto the bed, I felt the urge to push. The sensation completely took over me. For months I wondered, *How will I know when to push?* And you just do. Your body knows.

I'd crouch back into a child's pose with each contraction when I pushed; this seemed to give me the most strength. And I would cry out, literally like a roaring lion. My doula softly tried telling me to save that vocal energy for the physical, and I ignored her comment completely, furiously shaking my head at her. Thankfully it was midnight and there weren't women having their prenatal check-up appointments on the floor above. My noises alone would've scared them all away from having a drug-free birth.

And then only a few moments later, the baby's heartbeat slowed down. That's when I heard the nurse tell me to slow my breath and, "Okay, Hayley. We need to get this baby out." I had only been pushing for two minutes, and apparently, I only had minutes more.

I was told to switch positions from my back, to my side, to all fours with pillows propped for support; I was being flipped around like a pancake.

For encouragement, the midwife had me reach down and feel my baby's head when crowning—it felt like a soft, crinkled walnut.

His head was now out, but the cord was tightly wrapped around his neck twice and he wasn't breathing. I had no idea our baby was in danger, but Chris did.

I ended up on my back and was told to push towards the ceiling, which helped immensely. The midwife was also holding a twisted sheet and I pulled on it like I was climbing a ladder, as she tugged back. I truly felt like I was fighting for my life and the life still inside me, and not a fragment of that statement is exaggerated.

I was pushing with the power of my every cell, yet could not get the rest of his body out. To my later knowledge, he had shoulder dystocia, a positioning that caused him to be stuck behind my pelvic bone. That is why later, my eyes and face and chest would be dotted red from popped blood vessels.

Panic started to fill the room, and for a moment, I honestly questioned if I was capable enough. And you know I'm tough. Everything was just so incredibly intense and nothing like I'd ever experienced before. But as soon as I had a fearful thought, it would immediately dissipate because I was as present and "in the moment" as a person could be. It was like my thoughts were on such fast-forward, the words in my mind blurred into a white noise of concentrated static.

They had to break his shoulder to get him through me, causing a small hairline fracture in his newly formed bones.

I don't remember feeling the baby slide out like I imagined I would've. But I could see my stomach flatten as his body came out of mine. The space he safely inhabited for nine months, seemed to immediately deflate.

An entire day after I had started steady contractions in the comforts of my home bed, Everett came into this world.

His cord was ripped in half and he lost all of his meconium from the stress of delivery. He was blue and still wasn't properly breathing.

I was still on my back, excessively bleeding and empty. They had him on the bed next to me, with oxygen up to his face. There were two nurses, my doula, and midwife around him, so I couldn't see much.

Chris was telling me, "It's a boy, it's a boy" and I just cried, "My baby, my baby." It was equally terrifying and traumatic. I had no idea what was happening. *Did I do something wrong? Was I not strong enough?*

I had oxygen up to my face, too, which felt like a cumbersome disruption. It was so hard to breathe and I had no idea why a mask was over my mouth as I was leaning across the bed, trying to get to my baby.

My hands and legs were shaking like I had uncontrollable shivers. I was pricked with Pitocin in order to stop hemorrhaging, while they were still trying to get him to breathe. I was so scared and spent and felt lifeless: I honestly thought if I closed my eyes, I'd go to wherever it is you are.

They took Everett to a table and were rubbing him for stimulation. His color was still very pale, but he was now breathing. I could see, even from feet away, that his eyes were wide open and he looked so curious. My doula was talking to him, greeting him into life, and I said aloud, "His name is Everett," so everyone could hear.

The women were all talking with each other about transferring him to the hospital, telling different people to call different places, but they all stayed calm and collected.

For a brief moment, Everett was laid on my chest. I couldn't really see his face from how he was positioned, but held his little bum and caught glimpses of his eyes. He was still looking all around, trying to hold his head up. Chris was leaning right over us, and he and I were crying with joy and relief and some magic wondered emotion that I have no word or name for.

Our son was stable, but my midwife wanted to transfer him to the hospital because of his coloring. It was simply a precaution. So Chris rode in the ambulance with Everett, and I tried not to feel powerless when the two paramedic men held our baby and took him away from me. The need to protect my child surged through my body, and it took my entire reasoning mind to keep me still and steady on the bed, even though by then I was naked and bleeding and crying, only covered with a white bed sheet.

After a surprisingly few amount of stitches and delivering the placenta, I was able to be somewhat cleaned up and clothed and refuel with some food. One of the nurses made me an English muffin with egg and cheese and coffee, and it felt like a victory meal, even though my hard-earned prize was nowhere in sight.

I had to stay for at least four hours before leaving to be with Chris and Everett, so I had Allison come to The Midwife Center; it was a relief to see my sister walk through the door and straight onto my bed. And Chris was continually keeping me posted with updates and pictures from the hospital—Everett was thriving.

When I was able to be discharged, Chris came back to help with the process. And ever so slowly, like a deteriorating old woman, I got in and out of our SUV for the hospital drive, feeling blood rush out with every small exertion, like standing. But my condition didn't matter. I just wanted Everett.

We entered the NICU and I cried seeing him hooked up to cords and monitors. I held his little hand and everything I had just been through disappeared, and I got to breastfeed him right away.

His nurse had good news each time she talked with us. Every test they did on Everett, he passed with flying colors, so we knew early on that indeed our baby was fine. He just had a really scary start.

We stayed overnight in what felt like the hospital's version of a cheap motel. Up on the top floor, there were a few rooms dedicated to outpatients, decorated with two twin beds, a basic television, and a small adjoined bathroom. Every hour I'd wake up soaked in sweat that for some reason, smelled like celery, with water in my eyes, remembering the birth and wanting Everett. I felt detached, unable to properly adjust to no longer being pregnant without the evidence of my child.

Chris would guide me into a wheelchair and take us both down the elevator to Everett's floor. I'd nurse him and feel a little better, and we'd go back up to our room, only for the whole process to happen again and again.

Thankfully, Everett was discharged the next morning, on Chris' birthday. When we got home, I went upstairs, got undressed, and snuggled in bed with my baby boy. It felt so good to have him home. All finally felt right in the world.

I feel like I can do absolutely anything after Everett's birth, and I'd say that kind of confidence gives me a wonderful boosting start into motherhood.

I'm learning that nothing is how I expected it to be, but must trust that everything is how it's supposed to be.

JUNE 6, 2016

two months

Why do I feel so often that everything I know about myself has been slowly picked apart and why doesn't your Daddy feel it too? And my thoughts are no longer my own either. Streams of consciousness are abruptly interrupted by your needs and it's so beautiful and I surrender gladly day after day but something tugs from within.

All of it adds up to this feeling that the world has quietly shifted and I'm grateful, I'm so grateful...but it's like if you woke one morning to find the house you lived in for 32 years had been turned completely on its head in the quiet of the night and now the dishes are in the bathroom and the ceiling is sagging slightly.

-Caroline Snider from @the_wanderingeye

The days all feel the same...full of smiles, crying, stroller walks, and tight swaddles. And a lot of bottles and attempts to sit and rest.

My period has returned since I'm now done producing milk, thanks to binding my breasts, stuffing cold cabbage in my bra, and eating fresh sage—which has a fuzzy peach texture but tastes like it belongs on a Thanksgiving turkey. It's nasty.

With so many changes happening within my body, the concoction of hormones is convincing me I'm slightly insane. It is scary to feel so emotionally unsteady. No one ever talks about the "after baby" recovery, unless it's about getting their physical body back in shape. But what about the internal adjusting? When will my body chemistry reset from the making of Everett?

To my surprise, the parenthood initiation has seemed hard on my marriage. I never expected Chris and I to require adjustment post-baby, but a few weeks after Everett was born, I was honestly doubting our relationship, thinking that I had all the answers, and my husband was a pitiful person for not knowing how to soothe a baby to sleep or juggle five things at once the way a mother can.

He doesn't always listen to me about Everett, trying to do his own "techniques," even though I'm with the baby all day and know what works through many runs of trials and fails and final successes. So when he acts like he knows best or better, I feel like my job as a stay at home mother is pointless—like I don't get the chance to have the earned expertise in my "field of work."

This created the ingredients of our first parenting fight.

The more I argued, telling Chris not to let Everett cry himself to sleep, the calmer he got (how he does this I will never know), so I left the house. Not knowing where to go, I drove to the cemetery to see you. And I didn't care that I was leaving Chris alone with Everett. I so desperately needed out of there, I literally just walked out the front door, silently forcing myself for the first time, to trust my husband as a Dad. And trust that my baby would be okay without my care. For some reason, it's hard letting go of that maternal control.

It was only about five o'clock when I arrived at the cemetery, but the moon was already out, without a single cloud in the sky. Walking down the hill and towards the willows, I found your plot and laid my body down, as if the ground below was the most sacred spot within this time and space where I exist.

And then I cried, with purpose, cradling my head in the backs of my hands. I curled all ten bare toes into the green hairs of the earth, trying to mingle a piece of you and I together—the piece that you were once buried beneath, with a casket and shovels and funeral men.

Being a mother has proven to be so hard. And being one without you felt impossible in that moment. It often always does.

I asked aloud for your help. I asked where you were. I asked if you ever got to be with Everett before he came to me. I asked if I'm doing anything right. I asked when I'll feel comfortable leaving the house while Chris has Everett. I asked if my marriage will ever feel normal again.

When I expended all questions, I literally felt like I could properly breathe again, free and light. Within my clarity, I realized Chris deserves to have some insight when it comes to his son. And I'm allowed to have help from my husband—something that for some reason, is so hard to accept. If he watches Everett while I take a quick shower, I feel like I'm neglecting my duty as a mother. *Who am I to selfishly be away from my baby?*

All this time, I've had the notion that Everett is solely my responsibility because I stay at home, which is ridiculous. Chris is a parent, too. But I don't ever recall you shoveling us kids off to Dad so you could do something for yourself. Maybe I'm remembering wrong and maybe it's just a natural part of the generational gap, but

Dad provided financially, while you did the baths and naps and dinners and schedulings of every appointment.

So I feel like less of a mother—less capable than you, if I allow Chris to help me.

But I need him. He's always my center if I ever spin away, and in the past two months, I've spun and spiraled into this realm of mothering that feels so foreign yet familiar, because I'm shadowing the example I grew up watching.

And I can't yet tell if that's helping or hindering my person.

JUNE 29, 2016

It is said that women in labor leave their bodies, travel to the stars, collect the souls of their babies and return to this world together.

-Anonymous

Yesterday was mentally messy; I couldn't shake the constant background noise that seemed to be singing, *mom mom mom*, as it teased my ears and mind and heart.

At one point while rocking Everett to sleep, we were cheek to cheek and our tears touched together, rolling down between our faces. He was crying out of exhaustion; I was crying out of the absolute disbelief that you're not here with us, and needed you like never before in my life.

There's just something about having a baby that simply makes you want your mother.

In a strange way, I feel closer to you, now that I have a child and can finally understand just how much you loved me. But then other times, I honestly feel like I'm standing in some sort of endlessly open clearing, lost and yelling your name, desperate for you to come find me.

But in that moment as I bounced and swayed Everett, I tried to imagine you were there with us in his little nursery, invisibly aware of the "good job" I'm doing. And as he finally quieted down, I took a long slow breath in, wondering if you ever got to hold this sweet baby, somewhere, in some way.

I can remember during labor, right before I got out of the water and started to push, I was nodding off, sealing my eyes closed and no longer tensing or holding breaths during a contraction. With my elbow propped on the side of the tub, supporting my head with my hand, I felt like I was disappearing into myself. Everything even seemed muted, like someone had their hands covering my ears, with the volumes of voices around me set too low to hear.

Faintly, I could hear Chris ask if I was alright, and my doula calmly answered him, saying something about the transition phase of labor.

Now that I'm typing at my computer desk and not laboring naked in a bathtub, I can say with perspective that this phase of pain was an incredibly beautiful moment, a minute in time where you and I possibly connected, because I know my conscious spirit was no longer in my physical body anymore—it had to leave to flee the pain.

I am sure that I was "somewhere else."

Maybe that's when I went to the stars, to find both my baby and you.

JULY 25, 2016

three months

Because there really are as many answers as there are babies.

-a friend named Lori

I'm sorry we haven't talked lately. There's no set schedule to this writing—I just journal when I miss you, when my energy inside feels as if it'll combust like a whistling tea kettle, steaming in hot frustration because I cannot hear your voice respond to mine...because I cannot hug you or kiss you or see the beautiful face that will forever remain thirty-nine years young.

Now that breastfeeding has been resolved and formula feels both normal and accepted, it seems another hiccup has surfaced: I cannot get Everett to nap if it's not in my arms. He honestly wakes and cries the moment I put him down, after I've tried for what feels like hours of rocking him into a slumbering state.

And I'm scared to let him cry. I try to be tough and close his door and walk away while he's safe (but screaming) in his crib or Rock n'

Play, but I break every time. My natural instinct inclines to simply pick him up and make the crying stop.

This is a bit humiliating, but during a prolonged rocking rant, I came close to accidentally pooping in my Lululemon pants, having completely ignored my body's emergency call for the bathroom, because I was so determined to get Everett to sleep. You could say this was my breaking point, when I finally decided to let him "cry it out," despite how convinced I was I'd ruin his ability to grow into a secure adult if I did (thanks to the experts on the internet).

Anytime I'd hear him cry for more than five minutes, I'd debate and wonder and worry. *Should I get him? Is he okay? Is this bad? Is he starving? Is he lonely?* I was desperately asking other parents for their opinions and of course, everyone said something different:

I let them scream until they fell asleep from day one.

Oh no, he's too little to cry it out.

Wait until he's six months and you can start sleep training.

Just keep doing what you're doing. It will get better.

He needs to learn to sleep without you. You are allowing him to depend on you and that's not good.

He needs to learn how to self soothe.

And the best one I'd hear: *I don't know, all my kids were always good sleepers.*

Desperate, I started to keep a journal of when he ate, when he tiredly rubbed his eyes, how long he'd sleep when I held him, etc. And then tried to create somewhat of a consistent schedule, based on his internal clock that revealed repeated patterns.

It took about six miserable days of Everett screaming (and me calling Grandma constantly, asking for her reassurance), until he caught on, but he's now taking two naps during the day, in his own room, that's been equipped with blackout blinds and a sound machine. Of course, some days are better than others, but I finally have some time for myself—even if that simply means sitting alone on the couch with a cup of coffee and a TV show for company.

Besides for drying up my milk, allowing him to cry has been the best personal parenting choice I've made so far—he sleeps like an entirely different baby now.

During this sort of sleep training phase, I absolutely tore myself into pieces, trying to decide if what I was doing was okay.

I'd get on the internet and read a blog in search of nap advice, only to become bogged down on myself for not knowing enough like these "online moms," creating doubt and a new ability to ignore my intuition.

There is an endless amount of information online about sleep training and sleep methods and so much controversy over everything, from what your baby should eat, how you should swaddle them, where they sleep, and what kind of diaper is best. It's crazy and overwhelming and I'm officially done with Google. You never had it while raising your kids and somehow, all four of us turned out fine.

I've learned that when you become a mother, it's up to you to decide what is right, what is wrong, what works, and the fine lines between. You're forced to filter through advice you receive, understanding that there's no set guide, no necessarily right or wrong way to solve certain issues.

When you become a mother, your child immediately materializes into an actual piece of you, living outside your body. And it's scary to love an extension of yourself with such intensity because now your own happiness is always dependent on theirs, making my new concerns sound something like this: *Did he eat enough? Am I forcing him to sleep too much? Is he content? Did he poop well the past two days? Am I holding him enough?*

Up to this point, I've thought motherhood to be so hard just because you aren't alive.

But I'm beginning to understand that even if you were here, telling me to do this or do that, I probably wouldn't have listened anyways. And your advice may have not even worked because Everett isn't a baby that you raised. He is mine, and I need to be brave and strong and accept the fact that I AM A MOM myself. I don't think that has fully sunk into my identity yet.

Motherhood would still be hard if you were still living. It would still be hard if I had a million dollars or if I didn't stay home full-time. But this experience is shaping and changing me into a young woman I'm learning to love.

I have all the answers. I just need to stop thinking that *you* do, and *I* don't.

AUGUST 1, 2016
four months

I could not contain myself any longer
I ran to the ocean
In the middle of the night
And confessed my love for you to the water...

-Rupi Kaur

Now that my brain has created some expanded space, thanks
to more sleep and less worry about the baby, I'm being reminded of
myself, like the woman and mother within me are finally figuring out
how to dance together in a beautiful unison of a slow becoming.

I've decided to resume teaching yoga, something that has definitely
influenced this feeling of rooting into a motherly identity. It's as if
I'm taking some of my own personal power back, sifting it from the
innocent thief that is Everett, because I know he doesn't need
every ounce of thought and attention.

While pregnant, I was convinced I wouldn't want to work outside
the home. Now I can so obviously see the reasoning behind that

frame of thought—you never had a job, besides for your family. And I had always planned to do everything just like you, even without consciously knowing it.

Over and over again, it's proving difficult to not try and be the exact kind of mother you were, because I fear of what you'd think of me and my decisions as a parent. Sometimes I wonder if you'd think that teaching yoga just makes me a hippie—the very stereotype you once rolled your eyes at when I asked to buy a pack of incense on one of our beach vacations.

Do you think I'm irresponsible for leaving the house on Sunday mornings to teach? Do you think I'm selfish? Do you wish you would've had a little side passion that gave you the opportunity to keep your calm and sanity and independence from kids?

Questions like these seem like they'll always ache for answers, because without you here, I don't ever get approval. I have to constantly trust the self I am choosing to be, both as a mother and an individual, even if I can't hear you say how proud you are.

That's one of the things I miss the most—you were my encourager, the only person in this world who loved me the same way I now love my son. And while I've learned because of Everett, that a love like that can never fade or diminish or disappear in death, how do I find the love again if I cannot see it or touch it or hear it?

This old journal entry, written when I was nineteen years old, seems to answer that very question...

JUNE 11, 2011

We're on our family beach vacation right now. It's the second annual summer trip without Mom.

Just a little bit ago, I went out into the hot tub. No other surrounding houses could see me, so I decided to skinny dip, feeling unrestricted under the rain that had just started to drizzle. And then an idea to go down to the ocean overcame me, like I needed to—it's literally right in front of our house, only a few hundred feet away and below the dunes.

So I got a flash light, wrapped a towel around my body, and walked down the private boardwalk to the beach, all the way to the water's edge. I felt so brave in the dark, surrounded by the glow of the moon and stars.

When my feet met the ocean, I dropped the towel until it fell to my ankles–I was so worried Dad would somehow find me down there, naked, but when I stopped fretting, I turned my face towards the direction of the wind. And when I closed my eyes and got quiet enough, I felt her. Somehow in the breeze, she was with me. My feet were intermixed in the sand and cold ocean water, being pulled both forward and back by the water's current, and I was at one with everything that is–with myself, my surroundings, and my dearly missed mother.

I understood how small I am in comparison to what carries the stars above, but still felt like I was an actual part of the sky and the breeze and the sound of the water. And my mother is a part of it. Everything is connected in ways that I'll never be able to explain, but tonight for the first time, I truly accepted the unanswered, as I allowed myself to experience what was perhaps one of the most beautiful and sacred moments of my life thus far.

There was a time when I felt connected to you—I think the 2011 entry above is a testament to that. But it's like I hit a plateau, comfortable with what I've found in Chris and our home and this life we've started together. I never needed to continue working on my beliefs or "spirituality," because even though you were still gone, I was happy.

But when I lay in bed at night, I don't know where to pray to. I don't even know *how* to pray. Kneeling on my knees with closed palms has never felt right. And I'm starting to feel selfish, not able to give proper appreciation for the beauty in my life, because *who do I thank?*

I never really cared before, but Everett has changed that contentment.

His creation started what now feels like a personal search for you. I thought I was only going to write about daily motherhood without you, but it's almost if these conversations have accidentally begun to imprint the beginnings of something much, much bigger.

AUGUST 14, 2016

Be with me always-take any form-drive me mad! Only do not leave me in this abyss, where I cannot find you.

-Emily Brontë, *Wuthering Heights*

I finally feel caught up with Everett's age, and it accurately feels as if four months has passed since giving birth. The days and weeks used to drag on and on into what felt like an eternity of endless questions and not knowing how to get him to sleep. When he turned one month old, I honestly thought a whole equivalent year had passed, while on the contrary, all anyone ever said to me was, "It goes by so fast!"

As they say about motherhood: *the days are long but the years are short.* But I think "they" forget just how *long* those damn days are.

Everett was constipated last week and I blamed myself, thinking, *If I was breastfeeding, he wouldn't have this issue.* It's so easy taking responsibly for all your child's problems as a mother.

So I started making him plum puree in the hopes it would help, and he actually got some relief. Of course, he loved it; he's a little food machine. I know I'm supposed to wait until he's six months before introducing solids, but I've learned that all the rules aren't necessarily appropriate for every baby.

Sitting up in an unsteady tri-pod is his newest feat, and he uses little fists in between the hollow triangular space of his legs for support. He loves to snuggle and I still keep him close to me in the beloved Moby wrap when cleaning or grocery shopping. It's a big piece of fabric that folds and twists and ties around my body, creating a cocoon of support for infants.

Now that he's a bit older, I can wrap it differently so he's able to face outwards while still strapped on my chest. He looks like a fly taped to a trap, with his arms and legs free to flail about, as he visually explores the world around.

Today marks eight years since you died. And the date had me searching for your eulogy earlier, which I had kept tucked and folded away between the pages of my *Wuthering Heights* copy. That book was my most prized possession in college; I read it in my junior year's British Literature class, a time when Chris and I were dating and starting to become physical, during the sweet month of a promising and changing October.

I remember highlighting the passage that begins this entry, unable to believe how accurately the author's words described what I wanted so desperately to say to you. *Do not leave me in this abyss.*

But I want to share the eulogy because it feels so completely strange that I was the one who wrote and then read its words at the funeral, with a crowded room of people sitting in front me, and your occupied casket situated behind.

Part of me wants to scoop that younger version of myself up, the one who was just weeks past seventeen, and simply hold her. I want to cradle her body because that grief was so heavy. I want to go back and promise her she'd learn to live again...

AUGUST 17, 2008

My Mom is the most beautiful person I will ever know. For anyone that knew her, they'll remember the Jenifer who always looked her best with berry-colored lipstick and bright blonde hair, but there was obviously much more to her.

No one was ever stronger and more determined than my mother, whether it was about getting new carpet or having a fourth baby–she was relentless with a lot of nerve and beauty. She lived for her family, always doing everything to make our lives as perfect as possible, ensuring we were all happy. I know that we were her world, and I take such pride in being her daughter.

We all won't forget the things that made her the heart of our home, like the nicknames she'd call us or the traditions she was so good at creating and carrying onward. Christmas was literally magical every year, and dyeing Easter eggs or our fancy Valentine's day dinners, are among the things I will remember. She had a way of making everything better, always going beyond what was standard.

My mom was and still is surrounded with so much love. She always told me she hoped one day I would see what a wonderful marriage her and my Dad had. I knew they were happy, but when I witnessed the way he took care of her in those last months when she was really sick, I finally understood. I am grateful to have grown up with two parents who truly loved each other since their college years.

Once while scrubbing dishes at the kitchen sink, she told me I was to carry the lily of the valley flower at my wedding. She said if anything should ever happen to her before I got married, I needed to do that and think of her. I now know some day on that day, I will do her the honor.

Her leaving has created an absence in all of our hearts. But I have to believe that she left this world knowing she did her best as a mother, daughter, wife, and friend. What she has taught my siblings and I are lessons that we will carry all throughout our lives. I know she'll be guiding each one of us through our different paths in this life. We have her legacy to carry on and can always find comfort knowing we have her spirited strength to keep us moving forward.

I promise her I'm going to do my best as she always did. I promise her that I am still going to accomplish my goals. I promise her to always be a leader, not a follower, just like she taught me. I promise to be a good daughter and a good big sister. And most importantly, I promise to have her strength through my life and make her proud of me, always.

I fill up with pride when I read the above paragraphs. Honestly. I am so proud of myself and of my family. *We survived.*

And I did carry those lilies on my wedding day, freshly cut from Nana's garden. It's ironic to think back on our conversation about them, long before you were ever sick. I was sitting at the communal kitchen island and you had your back towards me, looking out the window while cleaning dishes. Your view was of the yard, of the very spot actually, where I'd eventually marry Chris in front of witnessing family and friends.

We said our vows under the willow tree you planted when we first

moved onto the property and into the house, a once tiny twig that in your words, would *grow as our family grows.* It towered over Chris and I, as I stood under its weeping branches with shoeless feet that peeked out from under my dress, promising my biggest yes to my best friend.

When he and I arrived at our honeymoon bed and breakfast in Maine, there was a lily of the valley bouquet sitting in a vase of water, placed on my nightstand. The owner there had an entire garden of them and I refuse to believe that was just a coincidence. And all my life, those flowers will always connect you and I.

I'm learning that those little signs aren't just luck—they're like small reminding tokens...my physical proof that you still somehow exist, somewhere.

But honestly, as beautiful as those signs can feel, most of the time I still can't fathom where you've gone, why you are away from me, or why your youngest daughter has only four years of her mother's memory.

Without my conscious consent, unguarded moments hit me, and I'll find myself silently screaming and outwardly crying in the laundry room while folding clothes, begging for you to come back to me and for you to come home.

SEPTEMBER 9, 2016
five months

She liked being reminded of butterflies. She remembered being six or seven and crying over the fates of the butterflies in her yard after learning that they lived for only a few days. Her mother had comforted her and told her not to be sad for the butterflies–that just because their lives were short didn't mean they were tragic.

-Lisa Genova, *Still Alice*

I feel so alone.

Ever since you died, I always had that awareness of loneliness—you were no longer there to talk about the things that only a mother could care about. I lost the person whose opinion mattered, whose advice I'd adhere to. But now that I have Everett, I sometimes feel like he and I are the only two existing humans, functioning in a world ruled by bottles and diapers and the scheduled clock—a world my husband and friends cannot understand, just as I cannot fathom how they go to work and make a paycheck and talk to other adults.

It's isolating as a stay at home mother, especially at twenty-five, when people my age are still partying and dating and finding themselves. And I don't mean to sound like I'm complaining, because I chose this life, and I truly can't imagine it all any different. But I constantly think how different raising Everett would be, if only I had you...if only I had your company...if only my son had someone other than his parents, that was equally in love with him.

I've been thinking of you constantly, as if you've become an invisible companion who sits on my shoulder, nudging your presence to be known during the ordinary every day moments—like while carrying laundry up the steps, or in the seconds my head hits the pillow at night—there you are. And my mind seems to dust around every seemingly vacant corner, constantly searching for a new but old memory of you I've yet to remember.

Like when I was a little girl, maybe four or five years old, lying in bed with you at the old house. It was still morning; your hair was messy and your face hadn't woke yet. I asked to put my legs "in the oven", which meant in between your sideways legs because they'd always be warm. And I played with your long hair, holding up the strands and pretending they were long neck dinosaurs from The Land Before Time movie.

Or when we were driving in the Hummer at the beach, just you and I. It was the last vacation we took before you died. From the passenger seat, I looked over at you, and can still see how happy you were, teasing with me about all the things we were going to buy at the Outlet stores, while singing "We're gonna have fun fun fun 'til Daddy takes the checkbook away," in the tune of The Beach Boys.

Or the moment I saw Dad, sitting on the couch with his hands over his head, listening to your wedding song, *For Your Precious Love.* You only had a few more days to live, and it was like he was savoring something, trying to permanently compress the feeling of you, forever in his head.

Memories will always keep you alive within my body, and even though they sometimes sneak up and surprise and cause me to silently cry, I now understand the ability to remember as a privilege.

I've never wanted to share the following with you, because part of me feels like it's not my story to tell, but my mother-in-law has Alzheimer's. She is sixty years old. And it is literally breaking my heart, watching the woman who should've been my second mother, whittle away before she and I really got the chance to know each other the way we're supposed to.

It seems that recently, the sickness is slowly becoming more present, even though on the outside, her perfectly aged beauty remains unchanged. A passing stranger wouldn't visibly know there are knots and tangles invading the intimate parts of her mind.

Chris doesn't say much about the disease, being the quiet man that he is. If I try to wedge some words out of his worrisome mind, he'll tell me a few things about how she's been or what medication she's trying—things like that, but will never go into detail about how it's emotionally affecting him. And that's okay, because I've realized he needs the permission to grieve in his own way.

I had to adjust quickly to the idea of losing you. The time between your diagnosis and death passed with the change of two seasons; however, my husband has to balance the evidential pieces that surface each time we visit his mother—a forgotten name, a repeated phrase, a sentence that doesn't fit into conversation...all while knowing she is literally fading into her already forgotten memories.

Alzheimer's is different than cancer. When you first became sick, the entire family rallied together and planned and plotted and conversed about opinions and options. Your friends divided up help with dinners and taking care of the two youngest kids. And I can remember you and Dad going to several doctors and specialists, trying to figure out how to entirely extinguish stage 4 breast cancer.

But for my mother-in-law, it could take years and years for this to progress, which is the most devastating part. No one knows how much memory she'll have left in the upcoming years. There really aren't options and there isn't anything to figure out—there's just time.

Lately, as I've been particularly feeling alone, I think of not having you, of not having Chris' mom, and not having the person I once always imagined being my mother-in-law, Mrs. Treml.

When I got engaged, I completely cut off my relationship with her, in an absurd attempt to move forward from previously loving her son. He was my high school sweet heart.

But she's the woman who truly guided me back to the surface after your death—the one who took me prom dress shopping and out to dinners, and who I'd call just to chat.

And at your funeral, she was my footing. She'd take me aside to make sure I ate and drank water and simply sat with me alone, allowing for a minute of escape from the continual flow of condolences I couldn't comprehend.

Having her friendship eased the transition away from you, and I will always love her for being a mother when I needed one.

But this inability to have a maternal figure, leaves me feeling insufficient because I can't give my child a grandmother. I know the factors are all out of my control, but that doesn't seem to lessen the guilt.

My child isn't a priority to anyone else. And I know I have help if I need it—I could absolutely call Terri or Nana or Grandma, but only you would drop your day for him. Only you would care how much he weighed at his latest pediatrician appointment.

Chris grew up differently than me, with two working parents and only one sister. He never knew what a houseful of kids on a Saturday morning looked or sounded like, or that it was even possible to support a family off of one income.

At twenty years old, only a year after we started dating, I explained to him that I wanted to stay home and raise a lot of children. Thankfully my demands didn't chase him off, and now, I get to watch him father our son, knowing that I somehow nudged this gentle man into a life that can seem so scary until you're simply living it.

So while I don't have any form of a mother and therefore not much help when it comes to Everett, I hope that these grievances will gradually force Chris and I to be united as communal leaders of a big, overgrown family. We will be our own help, dependent on each other. And we'll raise children who will wholly understand the meaning and importance of togetherness, as we create those mundane memories they'll always remember.

OCTOBER 4, 2016

six months

And if you've had a bad week,
Let me sing you to sleep.
Oh and I'll be there waiting when you get frustrated.
I know things are changing but darling I'm saying,
I've been here all along.

-Maggie Rogers, Dog Years

I keep listening to that song. It's been on continual repeat,
reminding me of you each time; as if you're somehow singing the
beautiful words to me, Allison, Cole and Tatum—your four babies.

On my routine walk this morning, it was playing through my
earphones, and when the above portion of lyrics were sung, I
imagined a time when you and I were still able to sit in bed
together, watching HGTV at night and drinking Salada green tea in
your big king-sized bed. The water mattress would mold to my
body and I'd be covered with that fluffy down comforter, swallowed
up and safe. I can still inhale the sheets and feathers and how Dad's

pillow always smelled different than yours.

Everett is now six months old. He and I are having such great days together, and I could not be more satisfied with staying home. I absolutely love it. I love being the one to witness everything he does. I love being the face that makes him laugh and coo and smile.

I never had a career—straight after college, I supported myself with teaching yoga and working retail at Anthropologie and babysitting. I hustled, refusing to take on debt for another degree, or work an office job that wasn't fulfilling, because I had bigger plans: I wanted to be a mother. I wanted to be a mother who stayed at home, just like you did, and that's the aspect of you I'm most glad I followed.

Staying home allows for the simple moments, like eating lunch each afternoon with Everett, to become the precious pieces that make up my life. He's becoming my buddy, and I know that I'm his too, just by the way he looks at me. No job or amount of money is worth missing that.

Because when I sit on the couch and hold Everett up above me, getting him to laugh and in the process, getting giggles out of myself, I feel you. I remember you. And I'm so thankful for the way you and Dad raised us kids, happy and all together.

You both prepared me for the beautiful life I have now. I got to grow up gently watching and learning the kind of existence I'm currently inhabiting.

It feels good and right to be back teaching yoga, and last week, I took a class where I was truly able to *let go*. I practiced how I used to practice, before being pregnant and before giving birth.

Somewhere within pregnancy, I forgot that I alone have the power to tune my thoughts and worries and anxieties out, and I alone can breathe my way to feeling peace.

On my mat, when I really tune my surroundings to silent, I forget everything. I can hear my breath flowing in and out of my body, and I can feel when it leaves, as it hollows the spaces where I've accumulated worry and clutter. It's like I'm dancing through the combination of movements, music, and the teacher's voice, simply able to *be.*

In the first year following your death, I started attending yoga once a week. I consistently went every Monday, to the same teacher—I was drawn to her beauty and insight and the natural way I truly became her student.

My mind bloomed like a little lotus flower, each time I heard words about spirit and energy and connection. And as time went on, I could feel my beliefs about where you were, start to shift and shake and rearrange into new form.

I'll never forget her once explaining: if you took a dead body and filled the lungs with air, pumped the veins with blood, and somehow started the heart, that person would not come back to life because their soul has moved on. Their body is now just a body, an empty vessel, because the energy has left.

From then on, I stopped imagining you as a spirit in the sky, displaced and far away from me; I was beginning to learn that your energy was everywhere.

I just don't know how to consistently reach that energy yet, but know it's possible—like that night down by the ocean, when I was absolutely sure I felt you in the mixture of sand and breeze and water.

Yoga gives me the permission to tend to myself, because even though I'm a mother now, I'm allowed to put my needs to nourish first. This is new news to me.

I was always under the impression that when you have a child, you as a person are put aside. That your needs come second, you say goodbye to fun, and sacrifice becomes your new daily mantra.

However, I'm learning that these "facts" aren't the truth—that you can be a mother *and* a woman, like two twined entities, gathered from the same string.

I'm continually learning to mix old habits with new ones, rearranging my beliefs and routines and the daily ways I get things done around the house, because I now have a human to care for. But that doesn't mean that I have to completely lose myself as an individual.

Last week I went out to the bars downtown with my entire group of friends, the same girls who once called you Mrs. Norris at our middle school sleepovers.

This was my first time "partying" since my wedding, so it's safe to say I had the night of my life, dancing with both friends and strangers, drinking as much beer as my belly could hold. I was reminded of how young I am, and how much I deserve to have a social life, separate from my family one. There is nothing selfish about that, an ideal I've had to somewhat shatter since gaining the title of "Mom."

It's hard to give myself permission to have that kind of fun because you never did. You never drank, not even so much as a glass of wine with dinner. You never left us kids and Dad and went out with just your girlfriends. All I remember was fancy couple dinner parties that the two of you would attend or host—which is fine and fun, but that doesn't mean I have to do the same thing.

And don't get me wrong. I am no wild child. I didn't mean to sound like I go run free every weekend and forget my responsibilities. But I have found my balance, finally embracing this experience of mothering.

I'm confident with my son and feel familiar again in my skin and in my body. Bottles and empty breasts don't feel shameful anymore, I don't panic if Everett cries in public, and I simply know how he works now, like I finally found the magic manual. That's all because I've learned to listen to myself, without doubt and without other people's input.

With this new little boost in confidence, I recently submitted an essay I wrote to *Mother.ly*, a website entirely dedicated to motherhood. And they accepted it! I was beyond thrilled to be messaging back and forth with one of the site's founders, sending her my little bio and a headshot I had Chris' sister take with her photography camera.

Because of this small success, I'm beginning to have faith in the blog I created months ago, which was recently posted to social media: now these private journal conversations between you and I are openly exposed, which is terrifying, but I know I'm supposed to somehow share these words.

My writing might just take me somewhere.

DECEMBER 29, 2016
eight months

You have plenty of courage, I am sure. All you need is confidence in yourself. There is no living thing that is not afraid when it faces danger. The true courage is in facing danger when you are afraid, and that kind of courage you have in plenty.

— *L. Frank Baum,* The Wonderful Wizard of Oz

A few months ago, I went to my primary care physician about depression, concerned about how much my menstrual cycle affects me. I know it's been a long time since we've talked—in our last October conversation, I left you with the impression that everything was on the upside: I was back to yoga, spending more time with friends, and really starting to own my role as an independently confident mother.

And I wasn't lying about any of that.

But the continual monthly circle of feeling fabulous and then equally depleted, is the exact issue I'm currently trying to address. Because I don't just get PMS and want to eat chocolate and cry at sappy movies a few days before my period comes. From the day I ovulate to the second day after my cycle starts, I feel horrible. I think my marriage is over, I don't enjoy staying at home with Everett, and I want to seclude myself in the house as much as possible, preferably within the confinement of my bed.

For the other fourteen days of the month, I'm brimmed with happiness. I look at Chris and cannot believe I ended up with a man like him. I love being home and accept it as a privilege. I shower first thing in the morning and do my hair and makeup, which makes me feel ready for the day. I don't want to nap and I'm able to stay up with Chris and watch our favorite shows at night. I am vibrant, both inside and out, and I mostly feel at peace with where you are from me.

My monthly moods have fluctuated like this since I can remember, but I didn't really figure out the menstrual connection until a few years ago. In prior attempts to "fix" myself throughout college, I took birth control off and on and tried different antidepressants, all of which left me feeling more hormonally crazy or in a confused fog of funk.

I never found a doctor that appropriately addressed these issues, so I was always under the impression that I was faulty or exaggerating. I simply dealt with the mix of symptoms, understanding that this is just the way I am, and luckily Chris understood and never made me feel like those shitty moods were my fault or my doing.

Pregnancy turned out to be wonderful because it meant an entire nine months, period free. Even towards the end, when I was uncomfortable and ready to deliver, I didn't feel depressed. I didn't feel anxious. I still really enjoyed going to yoga and taking the dog for daily walks.

Two or so months after Everett was born, when my period

returned, I questioned if I had postpartum depression like you did when Tatum was just a few weeks old. I didn't know what was normal to feel post-baby, which made me terrified and alone to figure out why I was stuck in such ebb and flows.

I gave my body time to find its natural rhythm again and for my hormones to stabilize. But after another few months, I had had it. I felt like I owed it to not only to myself to get help, but to my family, so I found myself at the doctor's office being written a script.

She suggested I have PMDD, which I feel like most teenage girls could be convinced of having. I'm embarrassed to even tell you about it because the term sounds silly, but it's basically just severe PMS. She said Zoloft can really "work wonders" with the imbalance, and of course, I went ahead and read online about tons and tons of women that felt the same as me, and how this medicine changed their life. I was convinced it could help me, too.

Within the first week of starting the medication, I felt thirsty all the time and a little nauseous, but once my body got used to it, I started to like how I felt. My period was approaching and I noticed a positive difference. I could feel myself getting anxious and then not care, so the anxiety would disappear without any effort on my part. Everything just felt like less of a deal. But the good stuff felt like less of a deal, too, and for me, that was a problem.

And during one normal night, maybe three weeks after starting the prescription, while sitting on the couch with Chris, I looked at him and said, "I don't feel like myself, and I know it's the Zoloft. I'm quitting it." So I skipped my next daily dose, and that was the end of it.

Zoloft changed a lot of things. Sex wasn't special and I had no appetite for intimacy. When I kissed Everett good night, I didn't get little tingly butterflies in my stomach, thinking about how much I loved him. And if I sat down to write to you, I didn't have anything meaningful to say because my emotions felt dulled.

It evened everything out. Things became flat, all on a leveled field, so while it took away the brunt of sadness, it robbed me of some of the good, too.

I came to miss my fourteen days of happiness, of singing in the car and loving every little inch of my life. And appreciating everything and believing in you and feeling confident within my mothering decisions and myself.

My dear father-in-law has said this to me on several different occasions: "You'll have the highest highs and the lowest lows," and when I thought about those words after talking with Chris that one night on the couch, I knew I wanted to feel both.

Because my highest highs really are worth it. I just have to accept this, letting myself feel those lowest lows, and know that they're not permanent. And I'm not completely against modern medicine. For the past two years, I've had a prescription for a benzodiazepine, but it's different than an anti-depressant because you don't need to take it every day.

I get my 30-day supply filled once every three or so months, and yet, I still allow myself to feel guilty for this extra bit of help. But if my body cannot make its correct neurotransmitters after ovulating, what's wrong with the occasional store-bought kind? I'm not less of a mother or yoga teacher or wanna-be naturalist because of this. And no longer do I want to harbor feelings of embarrassment or shame, simply because I found a successful and modern way to mellow out my monthly anxiety.

It's all a compromise. And with time, I know I can figure out a way to not fall so mentally downhill for two weeks of my life—I just have to commit to helping me help myself.

That sense of independence, or the silent inner idea of *I can do this*, has been within me since I can remember, always having felt like I had something strong scribbled onto my bones, different from my elementary classmates.

And I don't want to sound like I'm puffing my feathers, because I'm not. This isn't a conceited confidence, but rather a trusting confidence—the exact one I lost when Everett was a newborn.

For all I know, maybe everyone feels that same inner strength when they're young and I'm absolutely no different. I just always felt like I could trust myself, that the "me within me" was going to be my best friend, sided together on the same front, courageous and brave, for all my life.

When I was six or so years old, I was laying in my twin bed across from Allison's, staring at the Wizard of Oz puzzle that Nana had pieced together and glued for display on my wall. It was huge, comparable to the size of a standard kitchen table. Looking back, I'm surprised you let me hang it.

And I can remember before falling asleep, looking at Dorothy's red sparkly shoes, and for some reason, wondering what would ever happen if you or Dad were to die.

I feel like I shouldn't be admitting that to you because it sounds too scary a thought for a kindergartner to be thinking alone at night, but I can still feel the emptiness I imagined. It was a heavy sadness, a confusion—a life I couldn't fathom. The thought was so alarming, I tried to suck it back into my mind and forever forget about it. And perhaps I did, until your diagnosis.

Even though you were the one who became sick, I immediately understood my entire life was going to be different because of the word cancer, and I'd need to truly be my own brave best friend, then more than ever.

The mantras of *I can face this...I can do this...I am stronger than I know*, all burst to the surface and I quickly learned to embrace every bit of that strength I could. It was either that, or I would be destroyed during the last of my pivotal adolescent years.

Because of my past, I know a positive mindset can make a difference, but that requires actual work instead of constant medication. I know that my inner self is still in there somewhere, rooting for me to find steady happiness and fulfillment again.

After teaching yoga for six years and having all this knowledge about breathing and meditation, why don't I consistently use it in my everyday life to help cope with anxiety and depression?

I want to be that strong teenager who knew she was facing what she had once feared as the young Wizard of Oz dreamer. I need to find how I can remain positive and still believe in myself, despite how depressed my menstrual cycle makes me. Because no one has control of my response to it besides me. And no one has control of how far or how close I feel from you, besides me.

Moving forward, I'm going to be my own guide, while remembering that I have faced far darker waters than menstrual depression. And I have this feeling that finally tackling the whole "God" word, will do me some good. For a long time now, I've felt disconnected in this physical world, far from you and far from the spirituality I was beginning to find as a once college student, completing her yoga certification.

I think finding faith in something is essential to my well-being, because I don't want to feel like I'm fighting alone anymore.

PART TWO
14 ENTRIES

JANUARY 4, 2017
nine months

Little boys should never be sent to bed. They wake up a day older.

-Peter Pan

I came across that quote the other day, and reading it just makes my heart sink a bit. I'm finally realizing Everett won't always be this little.

In the newborn phase, I can still remember how slow every second felt. I'd think, *Okay he's two weeks....we're almost at six weeks... seven weeks*, etc. Now the days and moments and minutes just whirl together, and sometimes, I feel like I can't catch it all.

Being a mother can feel so fleeting.

When he wakes up from a nap, he sits up in his crib and waits for my routine retrieval. When I walk into the nursery I say, "Hi baby!" in a real high voice, and he'll flap his arms and smile. Happiness seems to beam out of his body.

So much of my thought and attention consists of him and only him. Everett gets to be the center of my gravity because he's the first child—his life constantly pulls into mine, and I find balance within meeting his needs. But what will happen when another baby comes along? How will I share that already attended space? I seem to worry about this more and more often.

There was one night years ago, when I walked past your open bedroom door, saying I was going over to my best friend Kati's house. I was sixteen, and rushing to leave because her and I had somehow gotten our hands on her parents' pale ale beer, which we planned to chug in the basement. That was the first time I ever drank.

But before I could leave, you wanted me to lay with you for a little. I crawled under the covers beside you and you looked scared, not quite sure if you should speak the words that weighed on your mind.

Our eyes locked and you said, "What if that doctor is right? What if I only have a few months left?"

I stared back at you as we laid head to head on separate pillows and told my truth: "Mom, how could you only live until July? How could that ever happen? You're strong, and you've been doing so good so far."

It had only been a few months since your diagnosis, and you were getting different opinions from different doctors. This was the worst one we had heard up to that point—the one we all simply refused to believe. The family couldn't fathom you only having a few more months left living on this planet. You were our mother, and *how in the world could anything ever happen to Mom?*

Water welled in your eyes and you told me I was your baby. *My first*, you whispered.

We both just cried and held each other. Just the thought of that night is like a thick coat to the throat, making my swallows feel as if there's chalk painted through my airway.

I can remember the color white: your comforter, sheets, and pillowcases were always white. I can still see how bright the room was, and hear the TV playing in the background. I can still smell you—that mix of Paul Mitchell shampoo and Suave coconut butter and fresh laundered t-shirt. I remember how your hair felt against my face when we hugged and held each other, both unsure of what was to come of our family, but trying our best to pretend we'd all be alright.

But I finally now understand what you meant when calling me your baby. You had that one on one time with me, for a few years before Allison was born; that's what I have with Everett right now, and I'm in no rush to change it. This time is special, and I'll never get it back. He will never be this little again—even Peter Pan agrees.

For a while, I was kind of scared each time I thought about another pregnancy. As a piece of conversation, people would ask me when a second baby was coming, or if we had any plans to flourish our familiar flock of three. And that would get me wrangling a bunch of no-right answered questions.

How many children do I actually want to have? At what age do I want to be done with babies? How far apart are Allison and I? How did Mom know she was ready for a second?

But I want to stop trying to figure it out, because I don't feel ready at all. I'm currently content, and for the first time in all my life, not galloping into the future. It is so wonderful to be where I am, with a happy and content baby, as I feel comfortable in my mothering skin.

No one is going to rush me, especially not myself. I'll know when the time is right to grow our family. *Right?*

JANUARY 15, 2017

You can create anything you want, but to do that, you must follow the principles of the law. Eliminate all doubt, and replace it with the full expectation that you will receive what you are asking for. If you are not receiving what you are asking for, it is not the law that has failed. It means that your doubt is greater than your faith.

-The Secret

With all that baby talk in my last entry, it got me thinking:

Before another little one comes along, I want to take a trip up to Maine, where Chris and I honeymooned, but this time with Everett. Chris and I have briefly talked about going, but kind of under the assumption that, yeah it would be nice, but we wouldn't be able to afford it, and a vacation would be too much hassle with a little one.

A shift has happened however, and I'm going to simply believe we'll be there, without letting all the details (like cost and travel and lodging with a toddler) permit doubt. I am knowing Everett will be on the Acadia beach sand, as I drop a pebble into the Universal pond and create the repetitive ripples of action that will get us there.

Something I've always enjoyed reading and learning about is the Law of Attraction. And it simply means that *like attracts like*, so if a person thinks positively, they are able to draw positive experiences to them—think of a magnet.

I used to set intentions and visualize and really trust that what I wanted would work out—like when we bought our first house at just twenty-three years old, despite everyone's doubts. I've just become really lazy in the way I use my thoughts, under the assumption that a prescription would heal my mind. In reality, I have the power to do so, and because I believe such a thought, it's possible.

The Secret is a cheesy movie that Dad (of all people) watched years ago, during a time following your death. Perhaps he was looking for the answers that would heal his heart, in any shape or form, even if they were "hippie" or philosophical.

He got all into the Law of Attraction, looking for front row parking spots when we'd go out for dinner, or taping to the back of his closet door, a piece of an American Eagle shopping bag that said, *Live Your Life*. It was like a little vision board, further fueling his attraction.

In retrospect, I guess that phrase was a reminder that his life needed to continue, even though yours wouldn't.

The other day, Beast of Burden came on through my speaker while I was getting ready in front of the bathroom mirror. Everett was jumping beside me in his jolly jumper, jolly as could be, and I started to sing and snap my fingers, swaying my hips to the music. I got him to laugh pretty good.

And as I sang the words, I thought about who I was prior to Chris and Everett and this life we've created. I thought about how the things I have now, were once only what I wished for. And I thought about the boy who got me into The Rolling Stones in the first place, the boy who knew you, the one who broke me free and showed me how to think differently. He taught me that it was okay to test and question what I was brought up to believe.

We were young, had no plans for the future or cares or responsibilities. It was *childhood lovin'* at its finest, and yes, it was easy to do. Of course as teenagers, we didn't think so, but we simply loved each other, and loving is always the easy part.

So I took that boy (and I say boy because the young version is the only one I know), and the love we once had, into my heart. I held him there as I continued to sing, thanking him for being a part of the ripples that got me here, to the very moment singing:

There's one thing baby that I don't understand,
You keep on tellin' me I ain't your kinda man.
Ain't I rough enough? Ooooo ain't I tough enough?....

I looked at my sweet son watching his silly mother singing her heart out, and when I heard Chris calling up the stairs to "turn that shit down" (ha), I held both my boys, Chris and Everett, into my heart as well, knowing I am one lucky woman to have arrived where I am, and to wherever it is I'm going.

You should've seen me, with hot rollers in my hair, Chris' City Sports t-shirt on, and my red lipstick, having the time of my life. It's moments like these that make me feel alive and connected to something greater than myself.

Becoming a mother has been the best thing that has ever happened to me. Even if someday Chris and I won the lottery and could have three houses up in Maine and all the riches money could buy, I'd still say the same thing.

And Mom, I owe all of that to you (and Dad, too). If you weren't the mother you were, I would've never known just how truly great the family life can be. Or what it means to be a mom, what it means to be the one who cooks dinners and changes the sheets and gets Everett after naps and makes sure Chris has his favorite snacks in the pantry—to be the lover of this household. All of those little things have become a part of who I am, as simple as they may sound to someone else.

So right now, I'm bringing you into my heart too, giving you all the love and thanks I possibly can. I am going to try my best to keep this positive, forward flowing energy alive, even next week when my menstrual cycle is going to challenge me.

Maybe I'll go look for a good new book, in the hopes that it will help keep my mindset right. Because I deserve to feel this good, always. And now, I'm suddenly remembering that that's both possible and in my control.

JANUARY 18, 2017

In the green of the grass...in the smell of the sea...
In the clouds floating by...at the top of a tree...
In the sound crickets make at the end of the day.....
"You are loved. You are loved. You are loved", they all say.

-Nancy Tillman, *Wherever You Are: My Love Will Find You*

Yesterday, Nana and Allison came with me to the grocery store. They ended up staying for lunch and even dinner. We had the absolute best time, and my heart still feels happy and content and full of love from the day we shared together.

After Trader Joe's, and Whole Foods, and boxed frozen lunches, the three of us snuggled on my couch, watching home movies back from 1992-2005ish. And thankfully, Everett took an exceptionally long afternoon nap, so I had the freedom to relax. The three of us laughed and cried and talked and argued about what we watched, what we heard, and how we felt.

It was special.

I haven't stopped thinking about you since we watched those

movies, though. You are alive and well inside my head, and I just want to take you out of there and hug you for real. Because seeing your expressions and hearing your voice, makes me remember just how beautiful and vibrant and fun you really were.

You know, I'd cross the earth ten times over just to see you once again.

I have written through twenty-three papered journals, a detail I know you know, because you used to read some of them when I was younger, particularly the first one I started as a freshman in high school. I kept it hidden under my mattress, and you weren't so good at replicating its exact position.

I can just picture you, tightly tucking my sheets under in that talented way of yours, while hitting finicking fingers against something, discovering your daughter's hidden secrets and daily dramas.

But you looked so healthy and happy in those videos, it's like I now need proof that you really did get so suddenly sick. So here it is. I was sixteen when this was written:

JANUARY 27, 2008

I don't want to be writing this at all, but I'll have to eventually. On Wednesday night, the 23rd, my Mom was diagnosed with cancer.

Grandma took Allison and I upstairs to my bedroom with Aunt Katie. It was dark outside. Grandma sat on the futon with my sister, and I sat in front of them on top of my little Ikea coffee table. When she said the word cancer, my mind immediately went fifty different directions. Now we finally knew the mysterious reason Mom hadn't been feeling well since New Year's.

I didn't say anything, just stared, and then once Grandma's words semi-set in, I cried and cried while she held me. She rocked me like a baby as I snuggled into her. I'm sure Allison was being held too, but I honestly can't remember.

I felt like I couldn't move my body. Aunt Katie talked with me for a little and then I asked to be alone so I could call Nana. I did, and I just cried more. There was no hope left in my body. My world crumbled into itty bitty pieces in a matter of seconds.

Then I called my best friend Stephanie and she came over a few hours later. I was still sitting on the floor and she came up the stairs and sat there with me, holding me and talking and crying. She brought her things to stay the night. Before we fell asleep, I asked her if we could say a prayer together, so we did, lying beside one another in my bed.

We got up early the next morning and my driver's test was still scheduled. I went, passed, and got my license printed. The whole time I was driving, I was in a daze, just telling myself to get through it...get through it. And besides, the diagnosis didn't feel real yet.

Once I got to school, the whole senior high was getting out at 10:15 a.m. because of a water line break or something of the sort. I remember Jessie, bright and cheery at my locker (like always) and me having to pretend I didn't just find out Mom was sick. I couldn't just blurt out the truth then.

She was still in a world I suddenly knew I'd never be able to come back to.

I got home and went to the hospital. Grandma and Papap drove Allison and I in his Suburban. When she and I were in the back seat, I saw Grandma put her hand over Papap's resting forearm, giving it a reassuring squeeze, like they were uniting on the same front.

Walking into Mom's room, I immediately turned around to Dad behind me and we stood in a spot she couldn't see us. He hugged me so tight and for the first time in my life, I saw him cry. I remember feeling like I couldn't stand up and he just kept holding me. He could barely get his words out, but he said his love for Mommy and me and all us kids was beyond words, that love wasn't a big enough word. He said that he feels so much pain in his heart for all of us and wishes he could just rip it out.

I was wearing my new chestnut Uggs and the Roxy thermal with turquoise hearts I got for Christmas. And for some reason, I know I won't forget those details for all my life.

Then I went up to Mom's bed and just leaned down to hug her. I couldn't help but cry. Seeing her look so weak and sick made this all so real. We found out what kind of cancer it was and I was relieved when I heard it was breast cancer. That is the cancer people beat.

We stayed until night time. It felt like the longest day. I can only imagine what Mom and Dad feel like. He has spent every night there with her.

I need to make the best of the days to come and stay positive. I've got the best friends and family and the best mom I could ever ask for.

That between time, from your diagnosis in January, to your death in August, feels like a figment of my imagination when I remember or read about it. You were sick so quickly, and then remember how you improved? You ate clean foods, continued your chemo, and we were all full of unencumbered happiness, trusting you'd be healthy again.

And then came that last beach vacation with just the six of us. I think that was the last time we were all together, still existing in the version of our lives that would soon be forever changed.

One night before we went out to dinner, you and I were in the master bathroom of the beach house, finishing getting ready. You put on a blue and white tie dye dress (the bohemian clothes were starting to come back then) with white heels. I argued with you, explaining how you can't wear heels with tie dye, that you have to wear a flip-flop or some kind of relaxed sandal. You took my advice and we all headed out to this seafood restaurant that was on the water. They served sweet honey rolls.

While we were all walking back to the car, us kids ran ahead of you and Dad. I'll always remember how you looked, casually striding in that beach breeze and holding his hand, safe and protected in your white and blue swirled dress. And once we were a good ways ahead, I turned my head over my shoulder, wanting a direct view of you.

In the time it took to tuck my wind-blown hair back behind my ear, I saw the disease through your eyes, rather than my own. I saw you silently wonder if you'd be here to watch your kids grow up. And never again until now, have I truly mourned your death through your perspective: through a mother's perspective.

The thought of something happening to me and having to leave Everett, feels so absolutely scary, my mind can't even comprehend the pretend consequences. Or the thought of being pulled away from Chris is equally frightening. Thinking how lost he would be...how sad he would be...how I know he'd try desperately to pick up the pieces with Everett and our house and dinners and plans and all the love I gave that was just gone.

For you, I feel so sorry as your daughter.

And I feel even more sorry as a mother.

I want to take the pain I feel now thinking about all of this, and rip it out of me, like Dad said on that ingrained January day.

How scared were you for us kids? How scared were you for Dad? Did you worry we would forget you? Did you wonder how we would all turn out? Did you ever think of Dad remarrying? Were you sad thinking about all you'd miss? You had to have thought about graduations and weddings and babies and birthday parties and family dinners...

But how could you have missed that all? There is simply no way that you did. I know with all the truths I can possibly feel in my heart, that someone like you would never leave.

A mother could never sever from her children. And now I understand that when something eventually happens to me, I'll never be gone from my kids. I will never be gone from my husband.

This is something I never understood until loving Everett.

When I read his current favorite book, *Wherever You Are: My Love Will Find You,* I literally choke up each time because it's as if you're saying the words to me. They remind me that you're everywhere, Mom. They remind me that you're loving me always, just as I am loving you always.

You never left, and you never will. You simply transitioned forward, without your physical body. And while at times that can still feel incredibly frustrating, I'm starting to believe that I don't have to look for you, I don't have to wait for you—because you are here...

in the green of the grass...in the smell of the sea.

FEBRUARY 10, 2017

ten months

Magic is really very simple, all you've got to do is want something and then let yourself have it.

-Aggie Cromwell, Halloweentown

Everett is developing his own little attitude and spunk. He's crawling pretty fast now and tries to get into everything, as he should be at this age.

I chase him saying, "I'm gonna get you!" and he thinks it's the funniest thing ever. Or him and I will play around my bed, hiding from one another.

His favorite time of the day is either after a meal, or after the bath. And if I walk into his room when he's supposed to be asleep, he quickly flops onto his stomach and pretends to be snoozing. Just imagining him doing it is making me laugh. It's hysterical.

He's fun. He's a pain. And we love him.

As I suggested back in January, I did indeed find a new book. It's called *Ask and It Is Given*, written by a couple named Esther and

Jerry Hicks, who are able to channel a spirit called Abraham. I know that probably sounds goofy to you—I admit, it even does to me, and I'm considerably "out there." But so far, their teachings have been about the energetic connection we all have to the Universe. And that because of our ability to attract based on thought alone, we are powerful creators of our own realities.

It's a mouthful, but I feel like I've finally found something worth learning and understanding—something that may help me feel both closer to you and more in control of my life.

And I love the word Universe "instead" of God. They're really both the same thing—they're our Source, but Universe seems to be less concrete in its judgement.

This is the basis of the book's teachings:

Step 1: You ask (your work).

Step 2: The answer is given (not your work).

Step 3: The answer, which has been given, must be received or allowed (you have to let it in).

So the whole *all you've got to do is want something and then let yourself have it*, makes complete sense. Maybe that's why I found myself randomly remembering the Cromwell witch spell from a favorite childhood movie—I simply understand it now. It's all about feeling good, so the good can come.

But step 3...the letting yourself have it part, is where I get stuck. I let my doubts and fears and other people's opinions hold me back from a few particular dreams, and therefore, pinch off the Universe's intelligent plans to place them in my experience, because I'm not *believing*.

While I've been writing in this journal to you, I have fantasized about creating it into something real and published, but always under the assumption that becoming an author simply isn't possible. *Who am I to think I can write?*

I used to talk about writing a book in high school. I remember even telling Mrs. Treml, while outside on their deck, eating a cook-out meal of homemade burgers and green summer salad, that I wanted to somehow make my personal journals into a story.

Anytime I'd research what it took to become an author, or openly worded my desire with anyone else, they'd immediately say how impossible it was to be published, how the industry is suffering, or how nobody wants to read a memoir unless a celebrity wrote it. And I let that all stop the start I was too scared to try.

I have this house that I imagine Chris and I and our kids in. I know what color it is, I know what the front door will look like. I can even see our dog laying on its front porch, tired and comfortable in an older age.

There are printed pictures of it hanging in both my bedroom and kitchen. And my Pinterest boards are filled with floorplans and furniture and finishes that speak to the whole feel of this dream home.

I've been writing in my pen and paper journal, too, details about the driveway and how many acres of land the house will sit on. I write about the kids' bedrooms and our yard and the privacy we'll have located high on a hill.

Because for the longest time, this house and land seemed out of our current reach and so far off into the future, I'd feel sad every time I thought about it. If I mentioned wanting property to anyone, they pretty much rolled their eyes, like I was considering buying an entire continent.

This makes me think of something called The Crab Effect.

When we visit your sister and her husband down in Virginia, I get to go crabbing with Uncle Todd, helping him out on the boat, pulling up the stringed pots, sorting through the females, the fat jimmies, and potential soft shells. And when it's time to cook them, he puts the approved crabs in a big steaming pot, alive, pouring beer and some special spice over their stacked bodies.

There's always a few that try to crawl out sideways, their legs trying to make impossible upward progress, while a crab on the bottom pulls them back down with the rest of the lot.

If I can't have it, neither can you.

This, is The Crab Effect. And I'm realizing just how much people do this—how much I myself even do it, when someone shares a risky idea they're trying to believe in.

My life depends on me listening to myself. Similarly, as I've learned, so does the way I mother. And my dreams depend on me, too—the ones that have slowly been woven into my soul, too scared to dare and surface...yet.

FEBRUARY 26, 2017

Give me the life of the boy whose mother is nurse,
seamstress, washerwoman, cook, teacher, angel, and saint,
all in one, and whose father is guide, exemplar, and friend.
No servants to come between. These are the boys who are
born to the best fortune.

-Andrew Carnegie

I took Tatum to Ohio this past weekend to visit Allison. It was a little sister reunion. We laughed and fought (of course), and talked about you and the things we each remember—all the stories, all the quirks, all the things we miss and still questioningly wonder about.

It felt like some kind of soul trip, even though I was only gone for about thirty totaled hours. That was the longest I was ever away from Everett, just enough time to get me out of the fog I'd found myself in a few days earlier. I wrote this in my journal the day before we left:

FEBRUARY 22, 2017

I am so tired. I'm tired of being tired. And I don't mean sleepy–I mean
worn out, exhausted; I am mentally spent.

Every single day feels the same. Chris wakes up and goes downstairs to make coffee. He and I say a couple things to each other, let the dog in/out and then Everett wakes up. One of us gets him, changes him and I feed him his breakfast. Chris goes upstairs to shower, gets dressed and comes back down, ready to leave. Off he goes to work, and a lot of the mornings when he's kissing me and Everett goodbye, I am mad.

I am mad that he got to have time in the morning to get "ready." I am mad that he gets to get in his car and drive off with no kid in the car seat. I am mad that he gets to have an important purpose for our family, making money and providing. I am mad he will get to talk to adults all day and sometimes even has the privilege of going out to lunch. I am mad because I feel like I'm useless staying at home.

I start the same routines on a different day. My surroundings seem to never change.

I am yet again alone, with a baby and dog.

I play with Everett for a little until he's ready for a nap and then get a bottle, lay him down, change him, get his pants back on after severe struggle, and close the door. This is my opportunity to get ready for the day, and I feel rushed because I know I'm on limited time. It makes me incredibly anxious.

I shower and get dressed, wearing the same pair of black Gap jogger pants I always do because I never want to spend money on clothes for myself. I pack the car if we are going somewhere, asking myself the serious question, *Should we leave the house today or just stay home? Should I go to Target for cotton balls and a change of scenery, or just stay home so Everett can take an easy second nap?*

Once Chris gets home, I am so relieved and so excited. But he unloads his book bag on the kitchen table, even though I tell him every day not to do it. His shoes come off, usually in the middle of the floor while the dog is attacking him with a happy hello. He goes upstairs to change and comes back down, opening his computer to finish work things up.

And I get mad again. I get pissed, to put it better. All the excitement I had to see him floods away, and I'm left questioning my role as a housewife: the house somehow already seems messy and cooking dinner and chasing Everett while Chris continually works makes me literally scream.

The clean I work so hard to keep, unravels in a matter of moments. And the dinner that takes forty-five minutes to cook, will be eaten in a matter of ten.

Being a mother is an endless and thankless job.

And I love my job. I love being the keeper of this home. I love being Chris' wife. I love being Everett's mother. But what about me? What about me? WHAT ABOUT ME?

I feel like I am always taking care of something or cleaning up something or carrying something or cooking something or worrying about something. My job is constant and yet I feel like if I stopped it, my family would be fine. After all, I only have one child. People keep reminding me of that, like my life is supposed to be super easy now and I'm doomed once more children come.

Does anything I do matter? Am I the only mother who feels like this? I am exhausted and tiring myself out for what? For what?

When I get overwhelmed and want a break, I'll leave the house for an hour or so by myself, feeling guilty while I'm gone because I'm "leaving" my family behind. And I'm so used to having Everett all the time, it feels weird to go out without him, like I forgot to put on pants or something. I'll even ask Chris if I can leave, as if he's my father and I need permission, because that way I'll feel less shitty about being out and alone.

It's just been a rough week or so. I don't always feel like this. I just had to get it out and onto paper because what I'm feeling feels so real right now. I trust it will pass. And my period is coming soon.

When I read the journal entry above about Chris and cleaning up and going out to Target, I'm thinking, *What the hell? What do I have to complain about?*

But I know you understand, as a mother, the moments when you feel like your job isn't enough. There's no boss at the end of the day that says, "Wow, you got so much done! You're my best employee!" And no matter how much I feel I've accomplished, there's always more to be done.

Mothering is never-ending.

I am learning how to handle days like the one I recorded in my journal. I am learning that no matter how many kids I end up having, what I am feeling is normal. I know I am okay. I'm more than okay. And not just throw this into mid-conversation, but Chris recently got a new job at Carnegie Mellon, so I know I'll have more help and less distraction on his part.

He plays with Everett as soon as he walks in the door, throwing and spinning and kissing him until they're both laughing out of breath. This is when I constantly yell at Chris because his bag is on the table, his car keys aren't hung up, etc. But the other day when I looked at the two of them playing, with the dog trying desperately to be included in their twosome forte, I thought, *Screw it.* Be thankful for a man like this because not every father comes home, unloads his work load, and plays with his kid. I should embrace the messy chaos—not try so hard to keep my string tightly pulled to its spool.

After being with my sisters this weekend and talking about you and our family, I was reminded of all that happened to us when you died...how Cole and Tatum had to have au pairs and learn to say goodbye to them when they returned to their homeland each year...how sad and lost Dad was...how confused we all were, about our schedules, and rides to sports, and our lives in general. I was reminded how empty the house felt when the lover of it left.

And at some point, while staring between the blurred highway lines that dotted the traveling Ohio drive, I realized that I'm an essential part of my household, too. Just because I don't financially support it, doesn't mean I'm not a main contributor. I know if I were to leave, this little house would dry up of everything that makes it a home.

All of your kids were "born to the best fortune" because of how you cared for us—because of how you and Dad balanced your roles. When you died, all the background things you did vanished into air, making your death even more unbearable. I came to miss our family weekend plans and those familiar sweeper lines on the carpet you consistently kept.

I remember in high school, on the first day of senior year, having to drive all the way out to Walmart for a special kind of binder I needed for my anatomy class. And then going to Target in the opposite direction, searching for the recycled soft-paper notebooks I loved.

Checking off my supply list, without you for a change, made me feel incredibly lonely.

Wanting to keep the normalcy of school nights alive, I made a family dinner that night. I chose crab cakes, but bought imitation crab at Giant Eagle, without knowing there was a difference. Dad said they were good, but I can still remember lumps and breadcrumbs and not much flavor.

Later I took a drive to clear my head. It was a long day, and it had only been two weeks since you died. And even though you raised me to be prided with independence, I felt like I couldn't handle what I'd currently been handed.

I was stopped at a red light and the sun was going down. I stared forward, with my hands frozen stiff on the steering wheel, and started sobbing. I can still feel the overwhelm, as I suddenly realized the new feeling of life without you. I needed your help. I wanted to ask you to get my special notebooks. I wanted you to take my overfill.

But I promise you presently, that I'll never forget what I realized that first day of senior year. I will never forget how much life changed when my secret handler disappeared.

I am a mother, and I will always be needed. I chose my role in this home, and I should never take that position for granted. And I'm certainly never useless, especially if I allow my house's upkeep to come undone at times.

For me to be the kind of mom I want to be—the kind of mom I *know* I can be—I need to gain a little more selfishness. I'd like to drop the guilt when I get away and alone for an hour, not just sometimes, but all the time. And I need to buy myself another pair of pants, or perhaps two, because I'm allowed.

APRIL 15, 2017
one year

I depart as air...I shake my white locks at the runaway sun,
I effuse my flesh in eddies and drift it in lacy jags.

I bequeath myself to the dirt to grow from the grass I love,
If you want me again, look for me under your boot soles.

You will hardly know who I am or what I mean,
But I shall be good health to you nevertheless,
And filter and fiber your blood.

Failing to fetch me at first keep encouraged,
Missing me one place search another,
I stop somewhere waiting for you.

-Walt Whitman, *Leaves of Grass*

My baby is officially one.

I can specifically remember the morning of Everett's birthday, because for once, he had slept past the sun. Its light filtered through my bedroom curtains, and when Chris and I opened our eyes, we were shocked to greet daylight. I stretched out under the covers, looked over at him and said, "Hug me," in my cutest voice. It's the one he loves. And we cuddled for a few moments, until he said, "It's Snuggies' birthday! Come on!"

We went into Everett's room, the video camera in Chris's hand, and switched on the lights, saying, *Happy birthday baby boy!* in somewhat of a unison. Everett had a confused look on his face, but once his eyes adjusted, he stood up holding his blanket, smiling ear to ear because his Mom and Dad were both there to see him. He couldn't have been happier.

After breakfast, we opened his presents from the previous night's party, hosted by my in-laws.

The birthday food was excellent, the company was comfortable, and Everett was the center of all the love and attention he could stand.

But I missed you the entire time. And it was difficult for Chris' mom to continually remember why there were so many people in her home.

I had a dream last night that Chris and I were at this huge outdoor party. I don't know what people were doing there, but it seemed to be a concert-like setting, with lawn ticket seating. And amongst the tightly knitted crowd, I started calling for you, saying, "Mom...Mom Mom...has anyone seen my mother?"

I sounded like the little bird in that book I read Everett, who leaves his nest too early and sets out in search for his mother.

You were still alive in this dream; however, the party was just too big, and each face I looked at, wasn't yours. I was scared, literally feeling this fear in my sleeping state.

And sometimes I still feel scared about where you are. Sometimes I really want to ask people, *Hey, do you know where Jenifer Norris went? She was that bubbly blonde with four kids—yea, that one—*

*the one who died of breast cancer right before her youngest baby
started kindergarten.*

But the reality is that no one truly knows, which is frustrating as all
shit.

There are days when I feel where you are, and I trust the certainty
of your existence.

There are days when I think it's all a bunch of nonsense—that you
really are just gone, unable to help me and unable to know Everett.

There are days when I truly cannot fathom the fact that I haven't
seen your fading face for eight years.

You never got to see me as a grown young woman. What would you
think of me now? I wonder if you'd be embarrassed that I wear
"mom jeans" and moccasins, not the tight tops and high heels
you frequently flaunted. I wonder if you'd be proud of the fact that
I'm a yoga teacher, that my hair is mermaid length, or whether or
not you'd think I was beautiful.

And you never got to meet Chris. That, almost above all else,
breaks me the most, you know. For some reason, I sometimes
picture how he'd look when saying, "You sound just like your
mother," as I pretend he knows the hidden parts of me that are
comprised of you.

But even though eight years feels equivalent to an eternity, in this
first year of Everett's life, I've learned to feel closer to you than
ever, even in comparison to when you were alive.

And each time I think of you, it's not so much in a sad way
anymore, but in a *my mother is here*, kind of way. Because you
don't exist as a winged angel staring down on me from heaven—
what I feel is much more than that; I feel you are here.

I don't know what better word to use, but *here.*

When I think of your face and your hair and your lipsticks and the way you smelled after applying suntan lotion, my heart aches. It makes me mourn to see you in person. Your physicality is what's completely finite, and it always will be.

But what's not subjected to limitations is your soul...your spirit...your energy...your life force. Whatever anyone wants to call it, because it's all the same thing. When we leave our physical bodies, our spirit—the very "thing" that cannot be pumped back into a body (as my yoga teacher once taught me), returns to the greater energy it came from and continues to exist. It returns to the *Source.*

A few days ago, I brought Everett to the cemetery for the first time, on what would've been your 48th birthday.

I felt like I was somehow finally introducing my son to you, allowing him to share my secret place, where a realm of pleasant serenity always awaits my melancholy mind.

We sat on your grave, while he kept pointing ahead at the lake, spotted with ducks swimming in repetitive circles. I'd watch when he swayed his feet in the grass, feeling the texture of it on his bare toes, as I myself have done many times before. It was hard to believe how close he was to you—like the earth underneath us was literally comprised of you.

Look for me under your boot soles. Because you are now a part of the same force that grew the very grass under Everett's exploring toes.

He will never know your pretty face. He will never fully understand how fierce and funny and fun you were. He will never get to hug you, feeling the love his mother has for him immediately double, because you're the only other woman on this planet who could come close to loving Everett the way I do.

But you will be alive when I teach him your constant presence— how there is no this place or that place, no death do us part. And for anyone who has ever lost someone, it can be incredibly liberating to imagine there is no heaven, no hell, and *above us only sky*. Because with that understanding, the idea of permanently parting until death can reunite, is nothing more than a human illusion.

With confidence, I can believe Everett will know you in a more special and profound way, than if you were still here to be in physical person when he blows out his birthday candles each year. And it will always be my responsibility to teach him just how close you really are—that we're all tied together in such intricately detailed ways, there aren't words to quite make sense of it.

MAY 4, 2017

thirteen months

You are Eternal Beings. And when you re-emerge into Non-Physical, you do not become less-than. You don't become nebulous, unfocused energy that just swirls around in nothingness. You assume that perspective of All-Knowingness. You remember all that you are, not just the personality that you were.
But when your daughter, or someone who loves you, recalls that which you were and approaches it from a positive vibrational standpoint, you can reconstitute that energy and be, for a moment in time, that focused energy.

-Abraham Hicks

When I have a little girl, I want to decorate her room in mermaids.

Random, I know. But I was scrolling through bed sheets on Target's website and stumbled upon a mermaid set, thinking how cute it'd be to have a little Maine themed room, with seagulls and sand dollars and white clouds pouted on the walls. I can picture it all perfectly.

And speaking of Maine, we have our dates set aside for this October. Instead of waiting for Chris to say yes, I simply took the initiative and started small steps, like saving my yoga money in a stashed envelope, booking our hotel, and gathering enough gumption to ask Papap, the vetted pilot, to fly us there in his airplane—which will be an experience all together on its own.

Everett is walking now. He hasn't completely committed to two feet, but he's been successfully taking steps and strides across the room. I'd say in a month, he'll be running around the yard, chasing after Clifford.

People keep saying, "Good luck once he's walking!" But I'm glad he's so close. I honestly cannot carry him everywhere anymore. My back and spine have several muscled knots, caused from heaving around my cute twenty-seven-pound ball of chunk.

I seem to be having more and more fun with him, the older he gets. Every time he learns something new or makes a first face or tries a new sound, it's exciting. I know and understand why mothers get upset thinking of their babies growing up, but they're supposed to evolve forward. For some reason, my baby growing just makes me proud, not sad. If he was my last, I think I'd feel differently, but the plan is that eventually, there will be several more children to follow.

We've been playing outside on our porch a lot. Chris just painted its wooden floor, and I purchased an outdoor table, along with a new three-wick candle to top its center. Maybe tonight we'll eat dinner out there, call it a romantic date. We're having pork chops and Caesar salad, tossed with Fodder's dressing recipe. I love making it and thinking of your Dad, the two of you together, wherever you are now.

Yesterday, Everett and I spent the day out at Nana's. She took us to a local greenhouse, where we picked out perennials in the welcome-back warmth of the sun. Nana bought me a lavender plant, and another little one called a "creeping jenny." I had to have it because of my middle name, and it's now snuggled in the spring dirt outside my house, ready to creep, I guess.

We then went to Home Goods and shopped for stuff we didn't need, but I enjoyed browsing the store while Everett sat in the cart, snacking on crackers and making eye contact with everyone who passed. He loves going places, observing and interacting with willing strangers who always *ooooo* and *ahhhh* over his blonde twirly curls.

Chris was already home when I returned, so I was able to swiftly leave for yoga while he handled Everett. I was grateful to go. I hadn't practiced for two weeks.

During my commute, I asked aloud if you'd be in class with me...I asked for some kind of awareness of your presence. Because sometimes when I practice, when both my mind and body are still and unified, I feel you. I swear I sometimes even hear you, like this flowing voice coming through me without a hinge of pause, and you completely fill me up.

And minutes later, when I walked into the studio, sitting on the check-in desk were lily of the valley flowers, set in a little Dixie cup. You might as well have been standing there saying, *Now how much more obvious do I have to be?* Because I know when those lilies show, it's you.

Right now is the only time of the year that their little white bells are in bloom, and they seem to be abundantly everywhere: a patch of them grow below a stop sign in my neighborhood; I found a wild bunch the other day on a walk, picking just one flower and taking it home with me; Nana gave me one from her garden with the roots still attached, in hopes that it will grow successfully in my yard; I passed a lady on the street today carrying some in a tiny bouquet.

Anyways. At the end of this yoga class, during the final resting period, I laid on my back with my arms draped up and over my head, physically exhausted, with my mind completely turned off. I was so relaxed, I wasn't even aware of my body. I was just *being*, temporarily existing in what felt like a balloon of bliss that was impossible to puncture. It was incredible.

Tears began to spill out from my closed eyes; I was overwhelmed at the feeling of feeling you, like your spirit had melted right into mine. You were real, simply having become *focused energy*, being called from my *positive vibrational standpoint.*

I suddenly understood that I chose you to be my mother, even though I always knew you'd have to leave me someday. It was as if something other than myself was funneling this thought into my brain for processing, and it pulsed through every fiber within me.

And Mom, if I ever got the chance again, I'd still choose you. For reasons that may never make sense, I was supposed to only have seventeen physical years with you.

No longer do I feel like my life was permanently ruined when you died. No longer do I feel like our family was cheated. No longer do I feel like it all isn't fair. Because those mind-sets only leave me vibrating low and helpless, far far away from where you currently exist.

I reason the weirdness this way: if my body could conceive and grow and birth a human, why is it so hard to believe that on some level, I can connect with your energy?

Before Everett, I had limits as to what I believed to be possible. If I thought I felt you in yoga, after seventy-five minutes of moving meditation, I'd dismiss it and think that's just my brain trying desperately to believe you were real for a moment.

But my child is the perfect proof I've always needed to have a little more faith in the unknown—to have a little more trust in what I *feel*, rather than in what other people tell me, or in what I've always been taught.

I look at Everett and still cannot comprehend that he was once never here. I cannot understand how he started as a tiny tadpole in my stomach, who grew to full baby size and then came out and literally through me, into this world. I have no words for it, but he's simply my evidence of an unexplained miracle. Sure there's science behind conception and birth but come on, really—how does that all happen and evolve and come to be?

I'm sure there are some people who think I haven't healed or moved on since you died. Because even after all this time, I still talk about your death and about missing you and wondering where you are. Maybe a few even worry if I'm doing "O.K." And I get it, I understand their possible concern.

But what kind of daughter would I be if I just accepted your death one way and one way only, never to think or ponder or question or strive to find more answers that continually bring peace to my heart? I may never stop all the wondering, all the searching.

And that very statement, has come to identify the biggest parts of my person; I am who I am because of both your life and death.

MAY 18, 2017

If all you did was just look for things to appreciate, you would live a joyous, spectacular life. If there was nothing else that you came to understand other than just looking for things to feel grateful towards, it's the only thing you would ever need to predominantly hook up with who you truly are. Appreciation is the magic formula you've been seeking.

-Abraham Hicks

This morning, Everett woke up before Chris' early alarm for work, and when it came time for his first nap around 8:30, he wasn't having any part of it. He didn't cry when I laid him down, but for almost an entire hour, made what sounded like bird calls, and bounced up and down on the mattress with his stubby little legs propelling him upward, over and over. I watched him on the camera monitor.

He then managed to get the lid off his bottle of water, soaking his sheets—luckily this time it wasn't milk or juice. I tried covering the spot with a towel, but that obviously didn't work, so I put the sheets in the dryer, and set out for a quick walk with him in his Ergo backpack. Just fifteen minutes outside in the morning sun was enough to make him tired.

So now he's napping, after I doused lavender all over his dry sheets in the hapless hope of inducing him into a calm slumber so I can write. (I think it may have worked.)

I haven't wanted to do anything lately. No yoga this week, and I backed-out on plans with a neighbor yesterday. I hate when I get like this, but if I allow myself to just feel it out, it doesn't last too long. I know it's just my hormones.

I've been tracking my cycle on a calendar and this allows me to feel a little bit more in control. I know when my high points of the month will be, as well as my low, and don't fight my natural rhythms anymore. This is when staying home feels like an elevated privilege, because if I don't want to do anything but watch movies and play with Everett, my chores and plans can wait or be cancelled.

I feel like a charmed woman to live that kind of life, and I'm trying to be even more aware of that fact, more often, through the newly learned practice of appreciation.

When I take a few minutes to simply journal a list of things I feel grateful for, it's like I'm literally putting energy into a virtual bank account, where the value just grows and grows, awaiting a withdraw from the Universe, who decides when I'll receive an unearthly coincidence—like seeing our lilies, or consecutively catching 2:22, then 4:44 on the clock. And these happenings are always my reminders that I'm doing good—that I'm keeping good check on myself and my thoughts, and my higher power is somehow confirming my efforts.

On days when I think negatively and skip out on the things that make my being feel good, I lose this symbolic "money" in my account. I lose energy. I start to slowly lose my beliefs about being connected to you and my surroundings. And it feels terrible, but I'm starting to catch that crabby version of myself—the one I want to sweep back under the sand and bury permanently. However, I think just being *aware* of my moods and thoughts is the start in changing them.

The song Dreams played in the car the other day, and I felt an immediate awareness of God or the Universe or Source, as I've recently been referring to "it" as. And as I sang aloud with my windows wound down, I trusted that when those lyrics randomly played on the radio after I'd been flipping through the channels, it was a sign from you.

An Irish rock band called The Cranberries wrote it, and the song seems to have been a tuned theme throughout my childhood.

I can still remember all the habitual Saturday mornings, when our house was filled with us kids and happy disorder. Eggs fried for bagel sandwiches, while the stereo loudly played, and you'd buzz around with your bare face, demanding Dad *to turn it down*, still dressed in one of his oversized t-shirts from sleep. And when it came time for The Cranberries CD, he would play his guitar along with the music, singing with all the emotion he could possibly muster, while Allison and I sat on his lap in our pajamas, unaware of our messy weekend hair, equally enthralled at our father.

He'd sing:

Oh my life is changing everyday
In every possible way
And oh my dreams
It's never quite as it seems

And even though being married and owning a home and having a child are a combination of what I once only fantasized about, I still want more. I want our property, I want the house we vision. I want chickens and fresh eggs in the morning. I want another dog. I want the natural smell of woods and grass and clean air to be what surrounds my family's home and life. My children will play in the earth, digging worms and running about the paths of forest that surround us. I'll have a whole corner of the house's landscape planted with your lilies and my creeping jennies.

That is my dream, along with writing this book to you. And all those things are impossible to ignore, like a little rhythm in my head, constantly drawing the little details into life, like what kind of tile I'll have in my powder room, or what our chickens' names will be, or what my book cover will look like.

It feels healthy to have desires so big, and to understand that there is no reason none of that can be ours if we just believe in it. I know when I speak aloud of these dreams, people are going to pull out that Crab Effect: *Well how much money would all that cost? Are you sure that's what you want? Won't your kids be lonely without neighbors? Aren't chickens extremely messy creatures?*

However, I'll now know to kindly ignore their concerns, because as I'm learning to appreciate what I have now, the things that can feel so unobtainable at times—like being published or owning property— are slowly becoming more of a reality and less of a dream. Because acknowledging the good that I already have in my life, *is the foundation for all abundance.*

As I'm wrapping up this entry, I just heard from my bedroom, the downstairs echo of a television commercial playing that very song, Dreams. I must've deposited a lot of good thought into my reserve funds today, in order to have received such an obvious sign.

I know you're listening to me; I know you somehow heard the above conversation and are already aware of all the beautiful things I'll create within my reality. And I know you're going to help get me there. Because it's not my job to find the exact path. It's not my job to figure out the details. It's not my job to worry about *the how.*

My singular work is to be in a vibrational standpoint that allows me to receive each crumb of the bread trail.

And the fast-pass to getting myself in that vibration alignment, is appreciation. It's really that simple. So along with continuing to write my gratitude lists, each night when I fall asleep, I want to be appreciative for what I have now, while thanking my Source for all it's putting on my path, as if this book and our house and that land, are already real.

Instead of begging for these dreams and praying that they'll work out, let me feel thankful for them, as if the things I imagine, have already come into fruition.

JUNE 1, 2017

fourteen months

And whether or not it is clear to you, no doubt the Universe is unfolding as it should. Therefore, be at peace with God, whatever you conceive Him to be. And whatever your labors and aspirations, in the noisy confusion of life, keep peace in your soul. With all its sham, drudgery and broken dreams, it is still a beautiful world. Be cheerful. Strive to be happy.

-Max Ehrmann, "Desiderata "

Chris and I celebrated our wedding anniversary last week, and Kati got married over Memorial Day weekend. I was lucky enough to be a bridesmaid in her wedding, with the special honor of reading a poem at the ceremony. My favorite excerpt from it opens this entry. I find every word so beautiful and true.

On the dance floor, between spilled sips of (not pale ale) beer and wine, I loved catching up with parents from my past but still present friendships, telling them about Chris and Everett. And when Kati and her newly named husband danced together during the last song of the night, I silently wished my best friend all the joy she could ever hope for.

Mr. Summers was so calm, clear and deliberate during his Father of the Bride speech. It got me thinking about the same-occasion speech Dad once gave, and how our father/daughter dance seemed to sum up all our past problems and discomforts and grudges and erase them, within the timing of a three-minute waltz.

Somewhere in our sorrow, him and I fell away from each other for a long time, filling our distance with fights and misunderstandings of each other's lives. I tried so desperately to hold onto you, while he tried just as desperately to let go.

I resented him for moving on so quickly. I was mad if he wouldn't talk about you. I hated him for not asking about my plans, where I was going, when I'd be home—the details of my life you would've known all about. And I couldn't stand that he was so angry all the time.

But when he danced with me on my wedding day two years ago, I was reminded for the first time since we lost you, that I was his baby, and he loved me and always would. I understood that his hurt and pain and anger through all the years before, was not because of me.

Hayley,

I hope that you and Chris had a lot of fun in Maine on your honeymoon. I wanted to write you a letter that you could open when you got back.

I want to tell you again how proud I was when I turned the corner and saw my beautiful daughter standing on the front sidewalk waiting for me. While I was walking you down through the yard and the song you chose was playing, I had a rush of memories from when you were a little girl flashing in my head. It was a magical experience. Everything I had done as a parent was all for that one moment.

The entire wedding was perfect from start to finish. If it were half the amount of people it would not have been the same. If it was at a venue, it would not have been the same. It was meant to be what it was and where it was. It was your vision manifested.

While I was emotional at times, I was not sad. I know this sounds strange but I felt like there was a dome of happiness and love over us. I know your Mom's energy was there running through everyone. She wants us to be happy and to love and that is the best way to respect what she gave us all.

When "Dreams" played right after the ceremony was over, I thought of you as a little girl on my lap listening to The Cranberries. And I'll always remember when we danced together to John Mayer, you looking up at me and saying, "I feel like I'm floating."

So many people were happy, laughing and dancing and having a great time. A number of them said it was the most fun they ever had at a wedding. All of the vendors were wonderful, and the photographer Veronica asked how she could marry into our family.

It was all worth it.

Have fun creating your life with Chris now. It's not easy but everything worth anything never is.

I love you,

Dad.

The day Chris and I got back from our honeymoon, Dad's mailed envelope waited for me, with the above note tucked inside. It was the first thing I ever saw addressed to my new married name.

Both the wedding and the letter changed a lot between he and I. It unified that we felt the same way; we both loved one another, and our past relationship could finally be put behind us. And the wedding validated to him, me, and everyone else who was there, that you were still with us all. Like he said, *you could feel it.*

Chris and I have been together for six years now, two of them married. Our anniversary was the 23rd of May, and that morning, while Everett was still asleep, I pulled out the journal I kept during the beginning of our relationship. I guess I was feeling nostalgic and in the mood to recount what feels like my own personal love story, written down in pen on paper.

OCTOBER 13, 2011

The time that Chris and I have had so far, in this little space of a few months, has been wonderful. I can't complain about one thing. I used to think he didn't show enough emotion, but it seems he just had to get warmed up to me. And I still haven't gotten over how attracted I am to him. He's embarrassed he has a hairy chest, but I've always liked a hairy man–it's, I don't know...manly.

Chris took me out to dinner last night. He texted me first thing Friday saying, "Good morning...are you free tonight for a wonderfully plotted out date?"

It feels good to be pursued and not the pursuer. I think this is how it's supposed to be.

I could tell by the way he signed his name on the totaled check, that he's good and true and holds no bullshit. Yes it's only been a few months since we started dating and we haven't even had sex yet, but I already catch myself picturing the kind of husband he'd be.

Looking back—or "reading back," makes me feel so lucky for how everything worked out.

I am thankful. And I know I am always where I'm supposed to be, even though I still cannot make up my mind about when another pregnancy should happen. I know the last time I talked about it, I promised I'd stop trying to "figure it out," but I've begun to feel guilty for how easy my life is, like I need to add on another child to create more work.

This is the best stage we've ever been in since Everett was born. Everything feels known, relaxed and easy, settled in a comfortable place. I don't even have to lug a diaper bag around anymore—just a bag with a diaper in it. And no longer is my son the pulling tide that directs every thought.

I'm not ready to occupy this new inner space I've found for myself, with another human. I need to trust that when it's right for baby number two, whoever they may be, I'll know. And in the meantime, enjoy this simple season of my life, while I continue to understand that you, the Universe and God, exist as all the same energy.

And as I learn to believe in my personal power to attract my dreams, I'm learning how to find you, too.

JUNE 16, 2017

Your inner ego will do everything it can to stop you from changing and growing, especially since you're attempting to obliterate the very identity that you and everyone else has come to know as "you." Sometimes emotional blocks are set up to try and stop us, other times it's physical.

-Jen Sincero, *You Are a Badass*

I've been wanting to talk to you, but never completed the past three or so entries I started to write. And the longer I went without finishing one, the easier it got to forget about how important these conversations with you are.

These pages have become so special; a somewhat sacred space, for just you and I.

I've debated on whether or not to tell you what I'm about to write, because it sounds so completely strange, but my lips have been continuously peeling for the past three months; it is unbelievably painful and uncomfortable. When I take a shower, all the skin on my lips turns white and literally falls off with the simple swipe of my finger, and I'm left with raw and red lips. It's held me back from kissing my boys, drinking from a cup, wearing lipstick, and eating normally. I've met my wits end, several times now, not knowing what to do after countless creams, two rounds of steroids, three rounds of antibiotics, and a lot of false hope from doctors and dermatologists.

It seems like no one knows how to treat it or what the underlying cause is, but I have to know I can get better, even if there isn't a "cure." If I continue to wallow and stare in the mirror and feel sorry for myself, I'm only continuing the momentum of worry.

But as much as I can know this, I am stuck in a cycle of starting to believe I'll get better, and then when I don't see results immediately, I'll think, *Why aren't I healing? What am I doing wrong? Why can't I figure this out? What doctor should I see next?*

I know I cannot die from this. I know I'm still in good health. And yet, it consumes me, placing doubt and fear and frustration behind virtually every thought. Many times now, I've pleaded and screamed and cried aloud for you, wanting you to help me, wanting you to fix this, wanting you to show me what to do.

Because I feel so absolutely helpless, out of answers and options.

Perhaps the Universe is testing me: *So you think you're learning to be energetically powerful? Let's see how you handle this...*

I actually had one doctor (out of the eight I've seen since March), tell me it would take an "act of God" to find the reason for their continual peeling. So how can't I help but feel like I'm being silently pushed along a path that's leading me towards the successful dreamer I dream of becoming?

Having this "condition" has left me with one question:

How did you handle a stage four breast cancer diagnosis?

Honestly. How did you handle the fear? How did you trample through the unknown of doctors and opinions and needles and chemotherapy? How did you go on each day, knowing you may not live much longer? How did you wonder what would happen to your four children if your sickness took over and took you away? Because I feel like I'm losing my mind, and I'm far from having the cancerous disease every woman fears.

What was it like when you lost your long blonde hair? What was it like not being able to brush it or put it up in a ponytail?

Still in an adolescent mindset, I was seriously convinced that your hair alone could be the winning ticket to save you, because people who looked like you, didn't get sick with cancer.

The fact that you were hip and beautiful and not-yet-forty, has always made me feel like you had more of a right to live than other mothers. I know that sounds terrible. But for instance, on my first day of college, every mother I encountered looked outdated, wearing too-big red framed glasses and clothes from Chico's, not your Caché. I mean, there's nothing wrong with those things, but even just the way they dressed, panged at my heart, making it obvious that you were literally one or two decades younger than these parents, and yet, you had already died.

You always felt like an accidental exception, as if somewhere, the cards were picked wrong, and it wasn't supposed to be you.

JUNE 23, 2017

I can soak up your presence in the wind
And as the trees sing in unison with the breeze,
I know you're watching over me, reassuring problems that
only seem to be.
I will overcome the void that has been left,
In my heart, memories I know will be kept.

-Me, written sometime after you died

I don't know if I told you yet, but Dad and Terri have been in their new house for a few weeks now. The old house (or as I refer to it, *your house*) goes on the market soon. I hadn't been there since it's been emptied of its furniture, with locked doors, awaiting the realtor to start selling and showing the space I grew up in to strangers.

So last night, I picked up Tatum, and together, we went to give a last goodbye.

We entered the house through the garage, which was open and bare, looking ten times its "filled with stuff" size. But it's just a garage, so it didn't necessarily look wrong, just different. The inside of the house though, looked *very wrong*, as if the whole thing had been flipped upside down.

As soon as I opened the back door, I made a right turn and walked straight into the dining room, seeing the now naked floral carpet and your custom curtains and the chandelier you and I picked out together years ago. I stood there, stared, and burst into tears—the kind of tears that make your mouth curl in a stiff position and force your whole face to contort.

I saw us all sitting in that room as a family, having one of our annual Valentine's Day dinners. I saw us hunting for Easter eggs, tip-toeing carefully because that was the fancy untouched room of the house. I saw the spot where you used to keep everything for special occasions, like painted plates, embroidered table cloths, and taper candles, safely hidden in a cabinet of furniture that was once great Grandma Jenny's.

And from there I walked into the entryway, seeing the ten-foot-tall front door you loved, arched at the top and made of solid stained oak. I pictured all the times us kids stood in front of it, taking pictures on the first day of school and waiting for the bus. Or all the times the doorbell rang and Tanner would simultaneously bark at whoever visiting car was in the driveway.

It was the entrance to our home, and never again will I walk in or out of it.

The family room was empty; no couches, no entertainment set, no coffee table. All that remained was clean carpet, with foreign vacuum marks and the brick fireplace. I remembered all the December mornings we had in that familiar space, the real wood fire crackling as Johnny Cash sang, *We've got that Chrismasy feelin' again.* Wrapping paper would cover every inch of the floor, and we were all full of love and health and the promise that everything would always remain as it was.

I walked upstairs and went into your laundry room. I stood there with my head gently leaned against the door frame, and imagined you still there, in front of the open dryer, folding clothes into neatly assorted piles, with the home phone tucked between your listening ear and shoulder, talking to either Janice or Carrie.

My room looked like a barren box, with no evidence of the sleepovers it once held, or all the times I danced in front of my dresser mirror, singing with the radio. I opened my hinged closet doors, savoring the sound they made as the left and right sides swung open at the same time, and remembered picking outfits for school from an abundant selection, quadruple the size of what I currently have now.

I saved your room for last. I hovered in the doorway and uncontrollably whined the words, "Tatum I can't," but she bravely walked in ahead of me, so I followed. I saw the spot where the bed once was, where you and I laid so many nights, watching TV and drinking that Salada tea together; the bed you'd be sleeping in every morning, when I'd come to kiss you goodbye before catching the school bus...the bed we were all beside when you took your last breath.

I cried in your bathroom and your closet, seeing you with a white towel wrapped around your head, getting ready in front of the vanity mirror. The linen closet door still faintly smelled like your Mary Kay lotion, and I literally stood there and sniffed the white wired shelves, trying desperately to bring you back again in some way. I even slammed the two doors together one last time, remembering the sound they made all those times I walked in on you getting ready naked, followed by your screaming.

Tatum went downstairs without saying anything, and I sat in the middle of your empty bedroom, knees bent, with my arms wrapped around my shins. I cried continually and when I could, simply said, "I love you Mom." I felt fine after that, like my peace had been made and my goodbye had been said. That space was yet another reminder of you I've had to part with, like your clothes and your car and the fading memory of your face, but relief flooded my veins once I got it over with and walked out of your room.

It felt like the last thing crossed off the "list of letting go."

We re-locked the house and left, heading to Dairy Queen, where we sat in my parked car, eating sweet frozen treats, talking about you. And then it started to rain.

While briefly in the attic of the old house, I retrieved a stack of papers that for some reason, I'd once hidden within the insulation. The poem that opens this entry was among this secret stash, along with the beginnings of a romance book I tried writing in ninth grade.

But the five-lined rhyme I knew to find, reminded me of how hard I tried to make sense of your sickness. After you died, I wrote so much. I read so much. I journaled so much. I tried many physical activities. I studied certain subjects. I did "safe" drugs. I moved across the ocean for half a year, and it was all in search of you.

I did everything I possibly could to bring you closer to me, and I'm thankful I had the healthy journey to where I am now. All the books I read, all the journal entries I wrote, all the yoga I've done and the runs I once ran, all the places I've traveled, all the philosophy assignments, all the fun mind-altering experiences, all the people I've loved: it has all been a part of you.

You've been a piece of everything, in a way I cannot possibly explain with the limitations of the alphabet.

You were the force behind all of my so called "soul searching," and instead of going off the deep end when things got difficult, I turned to you, my own personal guiding God.

I honestly don't know if I would change it all, Mom. I've come to depend on you in the form you're in now, just as much as I once depended on you when you were physically here. If you were to magically come back to life again, I'd have to go through an entirely new adjustment period, realizing that, yes I could call you and we could shop at Marshall's together, but my all-knowing guide would forever be gone.

I can let go of everything, including the house, but not the permanent presence you've become in my life.

JULY 26, 2017
fifteen months

But when we really delve into the reasons for why we can't let something go, there are only two: an attachment to the past, or a fear for the future.

-Marie Kondō, The Life-Changing Magic of Tidying Up

Everett is my best friend. I don't know if that's cute or pathetic, but it's the simple truth. He drives me frustrated out of my mind some times, but most of our days are mixed together in this perfect little orbit, where we literally dance and sing and play and have lunch dates every afternoon at the kitchen table. Today we ate grilled cheese sandwiches and baked herb fries, double dipped in ketchup.

He still doesn't talk yet, but is starting to understand me more and more. When I say, "Do you want to go nunnies?" he runs for the steps and heads up to his room for sleep. Or he'll walk to the couch when he hears, "Want to watch Little Bear?" It's his favorite show and he gets to watch a bit of it every morning while we sit together and eat muffins for breakfast. It's evolved to be one of my most-liked times of the day.

I used to hate mornings, because I'd wake up and start cleaning. But I have found what it means *to tidy*, and this will sound like an exaggeration, but the verb change from "cleaning" to "tidying" has completely altered how I feel as a stay at home mom.

Usually every Monday morning, for as long as I can remember, I've done a deep cleaning of my home, or in prior years, of my apartment shared with Carla. I always hated doing so much in one day, but consistently believed the routine best because *it's what Mom did.*

Now instead of one day, I've broken down cleaning into somewhat separate segments, choosing certain days for laundry, a certain day for scrubbing the bathroom, a day for grocery shopping, etc.

And each night, after dinner and during Everett's bath time with his Dad, I take a total of twenty or so minutes to tidy up the house. I wipe the counters, pack up leftovers, sweep the floors, pick up any toys, and make sure both the dog and rabbit have food and water, as I check off the little things I don't want saturating my sacred mornings.

I'll light candles throughout the house, feeling like I'm putting the space to bed, in the same way Everett soon after goes into his crib, with a book and bottle and blanket, retiring from the day.

No longer am I constantly cleaning in circles—something that literally comprised half of your motherhood.

All of this change was inspired after reading a little book called, *The Life-Changing Magic of Tidying Up,* which has taught me not only to clean differently, but how to throw things away.

By having less stuff—less toys, less clothes, less bathroom towels, less lotions, etc...the less I feel disorganized and anxious, because there isn't disarray surrounding my sight. I've never been a messy person, but when I began minimalizing what was stashed in our bathroom vanity, I just kept going, emptying out junk drawers, and pairing down the amount of occupied hangers in my closet.

I don't ever want to feel like my home and kids are drowning me. I mean, I still hit the de-wrinkle option at least twice, for every load of laundry that sits clean and waiting in my dryer. But I'm grateful to be learning about this "minimalism within my motherhood," before more children come along, and before we build our home in the years to come—it will not fill with mountains of toys that aren't played with.

The less Everett has, the more he seems to play. And when birthdays and Christmases and our versions of Hanukkah come around, I want him to be thankful and appreciative for his gifts, rather than simply receiving something else to add to a stack of stuff in a play room. Maybe I'll come to bite these words later on, but maybe not.

I've held onto a lot of shit, all in the fear of losing you. Without even consciously realizing it, I've been scared to even clean differently than you, which now, sounds so absolutely stupid, but Mom—I would've done anything in the world if it meant feeling just one more inch closer to you. And cleaning on Mondays allowed me to believe that was somehow possible.

So has ignoring any potential relationship with Terri. I've always fostered a focal of resentment towards her, because I felt like I was still able to choose you instead of her.

But since she and Dad have moved into their new house, it's been so nice visiting—no longer do I feel like I'm torn between your space and hers. No longer do I feel like if I'm kind to her, I'm going against you.

And my biggest realization out of all the tidy and Terri talk is this:

Nothing I do or don't do, here on this physical spinning dot in space, is going to put more distance between you and I, because there was never any separation to begin.

I've held back on discovering parts of myself because I was scared to lose you. I've been scared to parent differently, or clean differently, or to have fun in ways you never would've dared, because I felt I needed to *be you* in order to *keep you.*

I mentioned Carla's name earlier in this entry, and now I can't think of a better example to shoot this point as far as it needs proved, in order pass through my stubborn skull.

A few weeks ago, she and I decided to meet up and take a yoga class together. And before we walked into the studio, we sat in the back of my Honda, taking a couple hits of pot, laughing at the fact that there was a car seat and baby books scattered on my floor— the innocent evidence of how much has changed since we lived together post-college.

In the backs of my mind, I had to try so hard to shake that guilt, knowing you were never one to take personal time for yoga, especially in conjunction with whiffs of weed. But it isn't fair to feel so ashamed for having a little extra fun now and then, just because I'm a mom, or because I did something you would've never done.

These old habits, like being mean to Terri or trying to parrot your mothering patterns, have kept me in a state of resisting who I really want to be. I am beginning to literally feel it.

Do you remember that time when you were driving me to my SAT tutor and you pulled the car over, screaming and crying aloud, "I can't feel like this! I'm not supposed to feel like this! The doctor says this stress is the worst thing for me to have right now!" And you cringed as you said it, your hands gripped on the steering wheel with your chest leaning forward and over it, like you were trying to squeeze the frustration out of your petite body.

I didn't know what to say. I just felt bad. And I still feel bad because I wish there was something we all could have done to just calm you down a bit when it came to your job as our mother.

But what I *can* do now, is refuse to ever let myself get to that point. I strive for a much simpler life than you ever wanted: not as big of a house...not as many clothes...not as many cars...not as many kids' sports...not as many marked calendar days...not as many hair appointments...not as many any of it, besides the amount of love our family had.

I'll even admit that on my vision board, there's a picture of a little covered porch, that I imagine someday, will extend off my master bedroom—a place where I can walk out and onto, surrounded in such privacy from the tall towering pines, I light that guilt-ridden weed with my top off, fully knowing I'm allowed to *do me*, even if it's not you.

Maybe every woman at some point in their life feels afraid to alter from their mother, or maybe I just feel like this because you died, but I think the epiphany has finally sparked—I know I don't have to try and be like you to keep you close. And there is no more choosing between anything or anyone.

That feels so absolutely freeing to fully understand.

For the first time in my life, I *want* to be different than you were, finally not afraid of admitting such a thing because no more fear remains; I know I cannot ever lose you, because I never really did.

AUGUST 14, 2017
sixteen months

Everything circles and spirals with the cosmic heart until infinity. Everything has a vibration and everything turns together in the same direction at the same time. This vibration keeps going: it becomes born and expands or closes and destructs—only to repeat the cycle again in opposite current. Such is also the story of the sun and moon, of me and you. Nothing truly dies. All energy simply transforms.

-Suzy Kassem

I know I always write to you, "Everett is so fun!" but he really is. Chris and I are constantly laughing at him—his sounds, his faces, his mannerisms. It's incredible how much joy a child can bring to a family.

But his attitude is definitely starting to show, and little tantrums here and there are becoming more common. Today he flipped out when I laid him down for a diaper change, sniping the poop filled diaper and throwing it across the floor. We were both in trouble.

He got his first shoes, a little dorky pair of velcro slip-ons I bought him at Target. He prances around in them like an awkward little creature, looking more and more like a big boy every time they're on his feet.

We walk out to the car together when we're going somewhere, a process that takes quite a long time, but he is so proud to open the door and walk down the front porch steps with me and those coveted shoes. Our hands are always anchored together, and we move at a pace made for snails, but I prefer it over bustling out on a mission like you used to do.

You'd say, "Come on kids, let's go," in that *I mean business* way of yours, rounding up your troop for the grocery store or wherever it was we were all going.

I like giving him the chance to do things on his own, especially since it makes him feel so special. Maybe someday with more kids I'll lose that patience, but for now, I'm enjoying it.

Everett's current favorite book is *The Hungry Caterpillar*, a story I can still remember learning about in kindergarten. When he and I read it together, I'll ask him where the caterpillar is and he points to it. I love watching him understand things. He still doesn't have much interest in talking, but it's nice to be able to communicate with him in our own way. It's as if all the mornings, days and nights we've spent together, have created a bond that doesn't require a mutual language.

I like to think about when you and I got to spend our days like my baby and I do now—home and alone within each other's company. Somewhere I know I can remember it all, on a level I can't consciously understand.

But I got the most time with you, something that often makes me feel like your death should've been easiest on me, in comparison to my siblings.

Last night I decided to go to yoga. I couldn't wait to leave the house and get into the studio. But the entry door was locked, and class had already started. I got the schedule mixed up, passing my chance to practice for the entire week. I was bummed.

Defeated, I walked back to my car, trying my best to trust the night would fall into place unplanned, and of course, it soon did. Tatum texted me:

TATUM: I'm going through a weird phase where the fact that I won't have Mom is becoming more apparent to me and I just feel sad and I don't know why it's happening now.

ME: Want me to come over? I can be there in thirty minutes.

TATUM: Can you just come to lay with me?

And I quickly knew the yoga class was missed in a serendipitous scenario, because I had somewhere else to be. My thirteen-year-old sister needed me.

So I drove out to Dad and Terri's, passing the old house and its "for sale" sign on my way. When I opened Tatum's bedroom door, she was cuddled in her covers, and I joined her without a hint of hesitation. Her eyes were glossed over and red. She had been crying, hard.

Even with sad eyes, she is so beautiful, and I'm not just telling you that because she's your daughter and my sister. Her eyes and nose and skin and hair are a stunning combination, with a built body to match her beauty. Allison and I always tease we're pretty but that Tatum is the exception—she got all the good genes there were to get.

She explained it makes her upset how she can't remember you— that she cries about you but doesn't really know who's she crying about. But she understands that you were her mother and she simply wants you.

This is an entirely different way that you are grieved, one that is foreign to me. And she used that word, *grief*, saying it started when she was ten years old. Before then, she was "too little to notice you were gone."

While she spoke, she was laying close to me. Her hands were tucked under her face in an accidental prayer position and our heads faced towards each other. She was so mature, so matter of fact, and it became obvious to me that she was starting to question your absence in ways she never had before.

I felt selfish, across from her with the ability to remember you. I can remember your laugh and the songs you'd sing and the annoying way you stuffed tissues up your nose when you had a head cold. The beautiful blooming young woman who is still my baby sister, has none of that. I'd give anything to imprint some of my moments with you onto her. But I can't.

I can talk about you and tell stories, comforting her in the times she's feeling sad. And I can continually show her that just like Everett's favorite caterpillar, she'll find her wings, too, even without you here.

This morning started out slow. I felt low on energy, but not just tired—I didn't feel like being positive or grateful, the two things that help literally lift me up. And when I sat down to edit the previously written portion above, nothing came out onto the keyboard. So I closed my computer, got Everett up from the nap he never took, and headed for the grocery store.

While driving, I knew I was being a crab and knew I was capable of getting myself out of the funk. A simple shift in thinking would've worked: *I'm glad I have money to buy as many groceries as I need...Everett is in the back seat, happy as can be...my hair looks good today...my grocery list is neat and organized.* I was just too stubborn to make even that bit of effort.

Spreading good through my mind has really become that simple, but this morning it was like I wanted to take a rain check on happiness. *No thanks Universe, I don't feel like aknowledging positivity right now. Just let me be.*

And then I got a text from Mrs. Hapach, and as soon as I saw her name on my phone, I knew what today was. Jessie's mom messages me faithfully, two days a year: your birthday and on the 14th, the day you died.

Feeling like I connected the dots, I had linked together the day and my sad energy. I mentally changed my plans and went to Chipotle before grocery shopping. *Screw it,* I thought. I was hungry, and instead of the store before some lunch, I rebelled the intended order of my errands, trying to simply choose what felt best.

Everett and I walked into Chipotle, our hands linked together, and found our place in line. I soon realized the man in front of me was your old hair stylist, someone your friend Norma had recommended to you years and years ago. He was top-notch, costing a fortune for a cut and style, but that's probably exactly why you went.

For your first appointment, you took me along with you, and we both got our hair colored. I couldn't have been older than twelve. It was raining when we left the salon and we ran to the car, trying to keep our new manes dry. You sat down in the driver's seat. and with the gear still set to park, checked out your hair in the mirror, oooing on and on about it.

It's one of those simple memories that I'll always remember.

There's nothing special about it, but we were us: the little me, learning to be like her beautiful mom. It's a normalcy Tatum will never experience—it's exactly what made her so upset.

I asked this man in front of me, "Are you the owner of MCN salon?"

"Yes, have you ever been?" he turned around quickly to meet my gaze, happy to have a conversation in the long burrito line.

"My bridesmaids and I got our hair done there for my wedding." He looked pleased. And I added, "My mother used to go to you years back at your old location."

It was like I was desperate to bring you into my words and into the real world. Out of all the days in a year, today was when I needed affirmation that you once really existed. I wanted to say, *You did my mom's hair! Do you remember her? Her name was Jenifer and she was so pretty and one time we got caught in the rain leaving your salon together...*like a child's run-on sentence, a spewing out of letters that carried too much excitement to make complete sense.

We kept up a casual conversation, and at the register, he paid for me and Everett's lunch. I was so surprised, saying thank you several times, letting him know he made my day. He friendly patted me on the back, saying I made his too.

That whole incident turned everything around. I immediately thought, *That was Mom*, like it was an obvious acknowledgment or message from you saying, *I'm still here.*

I don't pretend to feel you to make myself feel better. When things like this happen, it ignites something, almost like an ah-ha moment, proving to me over and over that this energy stuff is real. That on the day you left this world nine years ago, you're no further from me now than you were before.

Thank you for the signs, thank you for the reminders. Thank you for the according accidents that brighten my days, reminding me that there is a rhythm tied into all things, able to connect what's both of earth and spirit.

AUGUST 25, 2017

Be softer with you.
You are a breathing thing, a memory to someone.
A home to a life.

-Nayyirah Waheed

I've been lazily in love with myself these past few months.

Since I don't have a reason to get ready for the day, majority of the time I stay in my pajamas with undone hair. Everett is basically the only one who sees me, and today, he's truthfully wearing a toucan print muscle tank, with rocket ships on his pants...we don't care what we look like around the house.

But I'm starting to fall short in the confidence I was once so abundantly full of because I rarely bother with a beauty routine anymore. I mean, it's fantastic being in the comfort of home with no bra, sometimes no pants, and a clean face. But I'm creating a yucky habit out of the mom life. Just because I'm not leaving the house for a job, doesn't mean I'm insecure or conceited for putting myself together.

And my lips have still not healed. My latest venture was seeing a holistic doctor, who put me on a restrictive diet that entailed no sugar, no wheat, no soy, no vinegar—basically a big "no" to all food groups. Determined, I followed her guidelines for an entire month, but with no results.

If the skin doesn't come off in the shower, it will dry and thickly flake, hanging off my lips like something that would be on a desert lizard. So how can't I allow that to affect my confidence? It is humiliating to go out in public and have conversations and be the social butterfly that at times, I love to be.

Chris and I haven't been able to kiss either, because it's too painful. And kissing has always been what's initiated sex for us—it's what allows me to feel sexy and powerful, able to pull my man into me, even if moments before he was staring at his laptop, absorbed in computer code.

But since I don't know how to heal my body, the only thing I can do to make myself feel better, is have a positive attitude. And if "getting pretty" in the mornings helps transform my energy, then I'm going to keep making the time for it, trying to trust that lipstick will once again be a part of that routine.

You set a really good example for me. I had a mother who really and truly loved herself. It was obvious for anyone who knew you. And I know you showered and dressed and naturally painted your face for no one other than yourself.

I used to do my hair and makeup without any clothes on, in front of the mirror. I guess I thought it was normal because you always did. But it forced me to look at my naked body and love what I saw, especially while pregnant and going through so many physical changes.

Now when I'm undressed with a view of reflection, the first thing I look at are my boobs. They've become deflated, like little dispirited pockets of skin, begging for the filling fat that my body simply doesn't have. Then I look at my teeth and the ever-growing gap between the front two.

Why is it so easy to think negative thoughts about my body but not positive? It feels weird to look in the mirror and say, *I love my hair. I love my stomach. I love my legs.* But without even thinking, I can look and say bad things.

And that's just it: *I'm not thinking.*

I had times in my life when I hated my body. I had times in my life when I over exercised, tirelessly trying to fight the voices in my head that said I wasn't thin enough. Or trying to fight the emptiness that was left after you died, treating my body like it was nothing, because I quite literally felt like nothing.

I had times in my life where I didn't keep my food down because I felt so disgusted being full.

When I'd throw up over the toilet, I'd think, *What would Mom do if she could see you right now?* But that still wasn't enough for me to stop.

I can't believe I'm admitting that all to you. Even for me to write such a thing seems like I'm making up a story about myself.

I can still remember how I'd hunch over the toilet and tighten my stomach, feeling the consumed food pour out of me. I can still remember how disgusting I felt...how ashamed and dirty I felt, when throw up would splash on my face, mixed together with toilet water.

I knew it was wrong, I knew I needed to stop, but I never did it constantly, maybe once or twice a month. I thought it was under control, kept it secret, and did it sparingly when I didn't know how else to cope with what felt like the loss of everything: my mother, my family, my father, my friends.

The worst was my freshman year in college. I was the loneliest I'd ever been. My childhood friends were no longer with me every day like they were in high school. You had been gone for just over a year, and the first shock of your loss was over. It all finally felt real. Everyone moved on with their lives, but our family couldn't. I couldn't.

When I would come home from school to visit, which was almost every weekend, you weren't there. Somehow, I still expected you to be. Dad would go out and I had no idea where he was going. Terri started to be present in his life and I couldn't handle it. I wasn't ready.

To deal with the emptiness within our house and family, I'd watch a movie in the basement of our vacant home and binge eat.

I'd eat goldfish and pretzels, mixed together in the same black ceramic bowl. Then some cereal and milk. Then a bagel with ham, egg and cheese, and I'd finish off with ice cream because it made for an easy exit out of my stomach. I would go up to my bedroom on the top floor and empty it all out, leaving me to feel evenly empty on the inside.

I just wanted you back. I wanted my family back. I was so desperate for our love and communal chaos again.

When I started consistently going to yoga, it taught me how to respect my body. I learned that my body was my vessel, and filling it with food and throwing up was not treating it as such.

Yoga forced me to sit still with myself and actually feel your loss. It made me feel my strained relationship with Dad and the changes he was experiencing. It made me feel the loss of who my young self thought was her forever one.

Yoga showed me that the past didn't really exist anymore, and no matter how hard I fought to get back to it, I'd never get there. It showed me that controlling my body through eating and exercising would never control the circumstances that took you from this world.

It taught me that I was worthy of love again and capable of giving it away.

I can proudly tell you now that I have not abused food since one night five years ago, when Chris and I got shamrock shakes at the McDonald's drive-thru. We drank them in his car and I threw mine up in private when we got back to his parents' house.

Afterwards, it was like everything finally clicked together, and I somehow had the strength to draw the line and stop forever. I was so ashamed and secretly embarrassed, but promised *never again never again* as I walked back into his bedroom. And I've kept my promise. I would never lie to you.

Having gone through all of *that*, I understand how beautiful my body is. I understand that it's flawed, but only when I choose to see those flaws.

If I feel good about myself and choose to say, "I love you," when I look in the mirror, more evidence will come my way saying, "Yes! You are beautiful. See?"

It's a shame it isn't easier to understand the power we have over our own lives. Why aren't we ever taught this? I have to read and search and journal and post positive affirmations on my refrigerator to try and constantly remind myself to *think before I think*. It's like I'm trying to rewire my brain.

All this good, loving, and positive energy that I'm trying to get absorbed in, starts with loving myself. It's an essential part I've skipped over.

I have you to thank for the self-love I've found—for the way you danced, the way you played, the way you dressed, and the way you carried yourself.

I have my yoga practice to thank, too. It is still what keeps me accountable for how my mind and body work in unison.

But most importantly, I have me to thank for the self-love I've found, and I'm giving myself all the credit in the world because frankly, I deserve it. I've internally overcome a lot. Very few people know about what I just told you.

I hope I eventually really do have a little girl, the one who will have her mermaid room, and get the chance to teach her how to love her body. To show her, through example, what it means to be confident and how to curate the courage to be herself, in a world that's always trying to change her. It's something you did for me— something I cannot possibly thank you enough for.

You gave me the zest I've always had within me, the vibrancy that I now want to claim back into my life. So no more holding off on the self-love, waiting for conditions to change, like my teeth or my boobs or my lips. Instead, let me simply alter how I feel about those conditions, knowing I am beautiful and powerful and capable, and that happiness should never be set aside, waiting for x y z to pass.

SEPTEMBER 20, 2017
seventeen months

*You need to raise the frequency to match the vibration of
the one you want to tune into. It's like trying to listen to a
certain radio station but tuning it to the wrong frequency.
If you have a hot and sexy date and want to listen to
105.9FM Slow Jamz, but set the dial to 89.9FM National
Public Radio, you're not only going to be Slow Jamless, but
you're more likely to attract a discussion about
immigration laws instead of attracting a relaxed and
candlelit body that's in the mood for love.*

-Jen Sincero, *You Are a Badass*

Everett has been a handful lately. He's still a good little boy but my
oh my is he stubborn, *just like his mother*, as Chris likes to
comment. But when he looks at me and says *mama* in a soft, sweet
voice, I just want to bottle him up and carry him around this size
forever.

In the mornings, when I do my now somewhat persistent "get ready
routine," Everett will stand at his bedroom gate, whining for my
attention. If I just shut my bathroom door so he can't see me from

126

down the hall, soon after, he'll stop his crying protest. And later I'll find him sitting content on his bum reading his (still) favorite book, *The Hungry Caterpillar*, having completely forgotten about the tantrum he threw minutes before.

I used to feel guilty closing the bathroom door for fifteen minutes, like *who am I to hide from my child?* But what mother doesn't sometimes hide from her children? I remember you doing it all the time. When Tatum was little, she'd hang onto your bathroom door handle and scream, and you'd keep talking on the phone and doing whatever it was you did in there, ignoring her charades for attention.

As a witnessing teenager, I'd think, *Mom is so mean.* Now as an experiencing mother, I think, *Mom was so smart.*

Whether it's making his lunch before I've had mine or not taking a shower because he'll cry in his room, Everett always comes first.

It is so easy to unconsciously push yourself aside for your child.

I wipe every booger. I change every diaper. I provide every snack and meal and sippy cup and bottle. I clean all the crumbs. I guide him down the steps. I take him in and out of the car seat, in and out of the high chair, in and out of the crib, in and out of the stroller. I do it all for him, all day.

And I would never, ever want to change that. I love taking care of him and getting to play and watch him grow during our lazy afternoons together at home. I'd wouldn't want someone else always wiping his bum or making his grilled cheese sandwiches. I just get swept away into the little world of Everett and forget about mine.

Even as a mother, I'm a priority. I don't know why this is so hard to both understand and put into practice.

On Friday, I took Everett on his first zoo trip. Allison and Nana tagged along, and we all had a good time. Everett just wanted to run around, his interest more concerned in the amount of free roaming space he had, rather than the animals. He did laugh at the sea lions, though, and we got to see an elephant get her bath; it was pretty cool.

But right before we left the house for our adventure, I had set aside ten or so minutes to buy concert tickets for the Sylvan Esso show that my sisters and I had been planning to attend.

A few weeks ago they were $25 a piece online, and not thinking the price would change, or there would be any kind of ticket shortage, I waited to purchase them—silly me.

Turns out, tickets had doubled in price. I immediately texted both sisters and they each flipped out on me, responding with messages like, *Why did you wait omg I am so mad I can't believe this Hayley.* And I knew if I didn't cough up the extra cash to cover the costs, I would be verbally slaughtered by the two of them, teaming up on me, two against one.

When I added the tickets to my shopping cart, they disappeared. I tried over and over, entering my credit card information and address, my fingers literally shaking at the keyboard because I was so nervous and in a rush. There's only a small window of time to check out when wanted tickets are in your cart. And we had to leave for the zoo; Nana was already on her way there and I was still at the computer in only my underwear and hot rollers.

Every ticket was sold out.

Too scared to quit, I found some sketchy website that had "4%" of tickets remaining, and after securing tickets only to lose them to somebody else, I tried one more time and somehow snatched and succeeded, getting the three I needed.

My total came to $228. Each ticket was three times its original cost. I wasn't even going to tell Chris what I paid—I was embarrassed to have made such an oversight mistake in procrastination.

My plan was to deposit money from my little stash of cashed yoga paychecks, secretly covering the charge to my debit account. But I texted him, saying the total and my jaw dropped when he responded, "No problem babes. Put it on the American Express." I just about died. And secretly felt super turned on and proud that my husband would say such a thing.

I'm happy to report the concert was worth both the money and anxiety. Oh did we have fun! I mean *fun*, involving a hotel room, two Uber rides, Jimmy John's, and enough laughs and petty sisterly arguments to remind me how incredibly lucky I am to have those two girls forever in my life.

We are so different, but literally made of the same *stuff*, fitting together like peas of the same pod would, perfectly right.

And as we danced in a triplet of twirled circles, singing our hearts out, I thought about how much I absolutely love them and us and you and where we've been, who we've become, and the places we'll be going with your guidance.

When we walked into Jimmy John's, this song called *Lean On* was playing over the speakers and Allison said aloud, "This is my favorite song!" Then in the Uber on the way to the concert, it was playing on our driver Sherri's radio and Allison looked at me, dumbfounded, like *how in the world am I hearing this again?*

And then the morning after the concert, we went to Brugger's Bagels to get breakfast sandwiches and coffee. While waiting in line, the same song played and with her awed mouth wide open, still painted red with last night's left-over lipstick, she said, "Okay now. This is weird."

It felt so obvious that you were somehow acknowledging our

togetherness.

Because when my energy is clear and positive and appreciative, like it was while with my sisters, I'm putting myself in the receiving mode, properly tuning my radio signal to let you come through.

So if I want to feel you, I can't believe you're gone and stay stagnant in misery (listening to National Public Radio). I have to get myself in the feeling place of knowing you still exist, of feeling appreciative for my family and my health and the particular way the sun shined (listening to sexy Slow Jamz). Because if I'm stuck in a sucky vibrational standpoint, I cannot find you—both ends of the receiver must match.

And it's the same concept if I want to turn this book into a physical collection of pages: I have to keep my vibration high, imagining covers and layouts and book signings at local coffee shops in my hometown of Pittsburgh. Or the seven-city book tour I "tease" about with Jessie, who has already claimed herself as my traveling companion. Then and only then, can the path to this success be directed.

I finally have a reason to keep practicing ways to raise my energy and feel better: you. Because the more time I spend consciously present, the closer I feel to you.

Oh Mom. I love you. I so absolutely love you and the knowing-feeling that you're here with me, like while uncontrollably laughing in public with my sisters until one of us peed through her jeans. Because that is where I find you: in the love I have for my siblings, in the way Everett laughs, in the fearless way I'm beginning to believe in myself and my capability.

PART THREE
16 ENTRIES

OCTOBER 3, 2017
eighteen months

If you are resisting something, you are feeding it. Any energy you fight, you are feeding. If you are pushing something away, you are inviting it to stay.

-Michael Singer, *The Untethered Soul*

I went to the mall a few days ago with Everett. He happily sat in his stroller, snacking on food while I shopped at Forever 21, my for whatever reason, favorite store. I bought a new scarf, a few sweaters, and a surprisingly functional tote backpack. (I've come a long way since my black Gap jogger days.)

On our way to leave the doors of the mall, I let him out of the stroller to run around—he must've thought he instantly became king. He trotted along a few feet away from me, looking over his shoulder to keep a watchful eye on his mama.

Refusing to stop his fun and having time to waste, we stayed, and I took him on the clear glass elevator to get to the first floor. He had a face of astonishment as he watched the world around him go down down down, looking at me and pointing and saying, *Ooooo!*

The elevator opens right up and onto the food court, and the smell of Chinese-style chicken wafted my nose, immediately making me think of you and all our times sitting there, eating after a shopping trip. I looked for our frequented spot, where the turquoise-topped chairs remained the same, and simultaneously searched for the sampling kung pao chicken lady.

I can still see the orange fried chicken clumps, on top of fluffed white rice. I can still taste the extra packs of soy sauce we'd douse our meals with, remembering how you'd tear the corner of the plastic packet off with your teeth and still manage to look pretty while doing so.

The last time I was at that food court, I was being interviewed for a clothing company called Buckle. It was the "cool" store during my senior year of high school, the place I bought all my Lucky Brand clothes in attempts of being a high maintenance hippie.

My possible future manager asked me question after question, and in between trying to give the right answers, I just wanted to speak out and say, *Are we done yet? I've got to get home. My mother is dying and I don't have time. Am I hired or not?*

You were sick at home, and it was only a matter of time at that point, like we were all just waiting for *it* to happen.

I never think about those last few weeks. I never really think of you being sick. It all happened so fast, that the small span of time can easily be swept into the back corners of my brain.

But because I felt so mentally stuttered when getting off that elevator and smelling that damn chicken, I knew something inside me needed released.

So when we finally got home and Everett went down for his afternoon nap, I went and found the journal I was keeping around the time of that interview, wanting to face this possible resistance, and therefore, give it permission to leave.

AUGUST 1, 2008

Well, cheer camp is all over.

I drove home with Stephanie and her parents, and while in the car, Nana called me to say the cancer had spread to Mom's spinal cord and brain. That's why she's recently been acting mean and confused and upset. And why I was the only one at camp without her parents picking her up.

I hung up the phone, looked out the backseat driver window, and cried quietly. Steph's mom reassured me that this would just be another treatment and that Mom would do great, just as she has been doing. I wanted to believe Janice. I wanted to believe Mom's best friend. But I couldn't.

When I got home, Grandma was waiting for me. After I showered and ate a quick lunch, she took me to the hospital to see Mom and Dad. I will never forget exiting the elevator, turning the corner, and walking into the communal waiting room where Dad and Allison were already waiting. Mom's room was twenty or so feet behind them and her door was open. All I could see were her legs, tucked tightly under a light pink hospital blanket.

Just by looking at Daddy's face, I knew something awful was happening. For a split second, before he said anything, I thought she had already died. I was so confused, I couldn't think straight or crooked or in any way, shape or form.

I was so scared and felt like I couldn't breathe. Dad talked me through it, and then sat Allison and I down, explaining to us that the cancer had spread. He told us the treatment options, something involving a box on her head and more needles and radiation and tests. And he said he had the option not to treat her any further.

Somewhere in all that, I heard she'd only have months to live, regardless of treatment or no treatment.

Even writing about all of this, days later in my journal, I still can't comprehend it.

Dad took Allison and I home from the hospital towards after dinnertime, and I'll never forget the drive home on the Pittsburgh parkway. We were in the BMW, the car Mom always said she wanted when she'd turn forty years old. Dad bought it for her thirty-ninth birthday back in April, probably knowing waiting another year was of no point because by then, she may not be living.

The convertible top was down, and the summer's day air was fading away as it hit my face and blew my hair wildly in all directions. The sun was setting and the city looked so beautiful. It felt so wrong to be driving home without her, like we were leaving her behind for good. None of us talked, but you could feel how hurt the three of us felt. How confused, mad, sad, angry and awful we felt.

I'm just in disbelief that my life has changed so fast. Prior to cheer camp, I thought the cancer was gone. I thought she was better, just meaner. Now she has limited months/weeks/days to live.

AUGUST 3, 2008

I heard noise down below from my attic bedroom and went to see what the commotion was about. Dad was giving Mom a bath at 11:30 at night. She has her days and nights mixed up. When he put her back in bed, she kept trying to get up, like a stubborn little child. Dad hasn't slept for days and I feel so helpless. He looks like he could fall asleep standing up. I told him to rest and that I'd stay with Mom for a little. She fought me the entire time, relentlessly trying to sit up and out of bed.

It's scary to think of what will happen in the near future. I could never have imagined any of this happening; not even the cancer, but just how it's all ending–her not being able to talk to us, Dad having to feed and wash her. She can't really even walk anymore and I'm not sure she knows who everyone is.

Her and I sat together at the kitchen island today while I ate an apricot cookie. She'd always buy them from Giant Eagle and she stared at me while I ate it, telling me "I was silly," in broken up syllables. I gave her one, and we each ate them together with a glass of milk.

Dad took her to Dairy Queen in her convertible and when they pulled into the garage, she had thrown up ice cream everywhere. I helped give her a bath afterwards. It's like she's crumbling apart, and we have to watch it because we love her and there's nothing else we can do.

On a happier note, I interviewed for Buckle today and got the job. I have tried to just keep doing normal things, like seeing my friends, etc.

AUGUST 14, 2008

Mom is doing really bad, not talking or eating or moving. Family has been visiting again, and it feels sickening to know they're all here to say their last goodbyes, as she sits in the same upright position in bed. Cole and Tatum are in Harrisburg with Aunt Katie and Uncle Ryan; Dad didn't want them here for what we think are the final few days.

And that's it for those entries. That night, on the 14th, you left our world, and never since then, have I stopped searching for you.

OCTOBER 15, 2017

All you've got to do is chill and follow the impulses that come to you. Pay attention: Source is using every conceivable messenger to get the point across. Be aware.

-Abraham Hicks

Oh Mom, Maine was so wonderful. We were gone for the perfect amount of time, just enough to make me miss home and shake me out of my same old routines.

It was so nice to not make the bed, not sweep, not do laundry, not cook dinner—I guess that's what vacationing as a mother feels like.

We stayed about an hour and twenty minutes from Acadia National Park, so early in the mornings, we'd get up, eat, shower and leave our hotel by 7 a.m. to make the drive in our rental car. Each day we picked somewhere different to explore: Sand Beach, Hunter's Beach and Ship Harbor were our three highlighted areas within the park.

Every place was more beautiful than the next, with mountains and changing colored trees and sand and rocks and trails of pebbles and moss. The air is so clean and beautiful up there. While in the woods with pine trees lining our paths, it smelled like a cinnamon Christmas.

Everett was in his glory on the sand, and I marveled watching him throw and toss sticks with the Atlantic coast behind him. I felt satisfied knowing I got my son to that spot, just as I'd imagined.

To see a vision manifest, is a powerful thing.

He seemed the perfect age for the trip, too; just old enough to truly have fun. It was like he knew he was the center of our attention, smiling at each of us while out at dinner, virtually saying, *You guys...this is just great!*

This trip solidified us as a family. It was our first vacation together (besides camping, but that doesn't completely count) and I loved how the three of us effortlessly existed off one another. I didn't have to ask Chris to put on Everett's shoes or make the twentieth peanut butter and jelly sandwich before we walked out the door. And when Everett would cry in the car, refusing to sleep but exhausted from exploring, Chris and I would carry on our conversation, not letting Everett's tantrum ruin our "fun."

For the first time, we felt like tried and true parents.

Before we had left for Maine, while packing, I wrote and tucked away in my suitcase, a post-it note that said: sign in Maine. I made the intention that I was going to find you up there—some kind of sign that would trigger my awareness, telling me, *Mom is with you.*

On our second vacation day, we pulled into the shops at Bar Harbor. Chris was unfolding the stroller and strapping Everett in, while I walked solo to the public bathrooms. In my few minutes of quiet, as my feet touched the beautiful layered brick sidewalks, I became amazed at the fact that I'd actually made it to Maine, having returned to the place where Chris and I toasted the official start of our lives together.

And just then, I passed a shop window that had a wooden whittled Blue Jay hanging on a corner display. It's a bird that has always, for some reason, made me think of you.

I felt like I needed to buy it, like it was "the sign," so without hesitation I did, and then shortly after, when I rejoined my boys, I started to think, *Was that it? No, stupid. It couldn't have been the sign. It was just luck.*

Sometime later, when we got into the car to travel to Acadia park, I heard Ace of Base's song play on the radio:

I saw the sign,

and it opened up my eyes,

I saw the sign.

I smirked on the inside, thinking, *Okay Mom...you win.* I mean, come on now. And my Blue Jay is now hanging on my vision board, where I'll see it often. It will be my reminder when I miss you, when I want so desperately just to call and tell you about my day or Everett's latest feats, that you are aware of me—that I am never alone.

NOVEMBER 6, 2017

nineteen months

Believe there is a great power silently working all things for good, behave yourself and never mind the rest.

–Beatrix Potter

I know I'm starting to sound crazy with the amount of times I tell you about the Universe. But I'd equate what I've been feeling the past few months as when people "find God," like some kind of internal awakening into finally believing something greater than myself exists.

And as a small side effect, I am becoming more aware of my surroundings, feeling like a literal part of it all. I notice the sky, the clouds, the temperature outside, and the way the cold wind feels on my cheeks. I am becoming more connected and more appreciative for all the things the Universe does to keep this planet spinning round and round.

Chris walked into the guest bedroom the other night while I was typing to you. He took one look at my desk area and said, "Jesus, it's like a serial killer's plotting in here."

One of the walls is decorated with quotes and plans and goals for this journal, everything but the push pins and red string to link together my ideas.

This writing adventure feels about half way through, having reached a point where I'm ready to whip out my map and see which direction the next summit is. Because I am ready for it. The hardest parts may be ahead, such as completing the actual book and somehow finding a publisher, but I've come this far and believe in it all too much to simply stop, put my gear down and turn around.

Right now, ideas and inspiration are essential, and the more time I spend with my mind quiet (I've finally been trying meditation), my words appreciative and my feelings positive, the more answers keep appearing in my experience—like "the way" is simply unfolding if I don't worry or doubt or get too ahead of myself.

One of my favorite authors, Jen Sincero (whose quotes I've included in here before—I kind of have a crush on her), came out with a new book this year called, *You Are a Badass at Making Money*. I would see it in Half Price Books each month when I frequented the store, sitting on the shelf with a bright green colored cover. It always caught my attention but I'd ignore it—like literally look away from the title, thinking, *A book about money? Not interested.*

Then I read an online article that mentioned her and the new book release. And a few days after that, my sister-in-law sent a text, saying how much she was enjoying the book on tape. And then a yoga student told me they were reading it.

Ignoring or feeling resistance towards this book, was like a blinking light, alarming my body that something is off, and by repeatedly putting it into my experience, the Universe was saying, *Could you please just read the damn thing?*

So on a whim one afternoon, deciding finally to listen to the signs, I got Everett and myself dressed for a bookstore outing. While at the register checking out Sincero's book, I asked the salesman if he had *I Am Yoga*, a children's story that Jessie recently recommended for Everett. Unfortunately, there were no copies left, so I scooted on out and returned home, only to find an Amazon package had been dropped off on my doorstep.

It was a copy of *I Am Yoga*. Being the giving friend that she is, she'd sent it to me (well, Everett) for no special reason.

I felt lit up, really and truly, because the coincidence was so cool to experience. The timing of it was effortlessly perfect, assuring me I followed my intuition correctly with the purchase of the badass book.

Not to my surprise, it was an incredible read. And I believe it allowed me to uncover the root of my resistance towards money— the very reason I perpetually refused to read this book in the first place...

Just because I am a stay at home mom like you were, doesn't mean I'm not capable or worthy enough or not supposed to make money for my family. I never saw you cash a paycheck, and therefore, never imagined myself doing it either. I earn a little with teaching yoga, but that's my "play" money. I need to start thinking bigger, so that the escrow earnings to be brought forth from this journal, can actually make it to my bank account someday.

So with yet another emblem added to my vision board, I wrote and attached a note that says:

We will be able to afford all the things and experiences required to fully live our most authentic life.

I have no idea just how much I'll financially contribute to the makings of this authentic life, but I now understand that it's at least possible, if I allow myself to dream a little differently than you did.

And after I finished the very last page of *You Are a Badass at Making Money,* I felt compelled to visit Sincero's website, in the search for her book tour dates. And while I was disappointed to have missed all the book signings for 2017, I clicked some link and landed on a page that advertised her very own book proposal course—the (very) big piece of work that is basically your sales pitch for literary agents and publishers.

Even though I immediately felt this course was my next step, the more I looked into it, reading testimonials and the finer details, I could hear my thoughts: *This might be a rip off...Chris will think it's a lot of money...are you sure you want to write a proposal?* But that is simply fear setting in. That's discomfort in the unknown. That's me not believing in something that was put on my path by the Universe to directly help me out if I'm serious about this book.

Because my faith in the Universe (and therefore you), depends on this dream becoming a reality. It depends on me believing I can publish this journal and make something of it. If these words become something real and concrete in a stranger's hands, it will be proof that there really is a great power, silently working things out for me and everyone else. Because after all, *I* decide if my writing will be a success. *I* decide if our dream property is already real, sitting and waiting for us.

In order to move further forward, things are going to have to get uncomfortable—otherwise nothing will change and I won't propel to where I want to go.

This all has me thinking of a question I once highlighted in the original *You Are a Badass* book:

Is your fear greater than your faith in the unknown (and yourself)?

Or is your faith in the unknown (and yourself) greater than your fear?

My faith will be greater than my fear.

So even though this feels risky and scary, I'm going to purchase the $147 online book proposal course and see where it takes me. If I hadn't bought the book...if I hadn't listened to the impulse to search her site...if I hadn't recognized that familiar fear trying to squash change, I'd remain stagnant and therefore sad, because I'd literally be resisting the person my inner-being already knows I am.

DECEMBER 8, 2017
twenty months

If we look at the path we do not see the sky. We are earth people on a spiritual journey to the stars. Our quest, our earth walk, is to look within, to know who we are, to see we are connected to all things and that there is no separation, only in the mind.

–Native American, source unknown

We are in a happy phase right now, here at the Pearlman home. I love this cradled in comfort time of year, right after Thanksgiving and weeks before Christmas, when the weather is cool but not yet slushed with snow, and that familiar anticipation awaits the happy season.

And I especially love the parties and traditions and togetherness, but ever since you transitioned from this world, Christmas has never been the same, even after all these years.

The first December came only months after you died. I ordered and bought and taped and wrapped, seventy-two presents for us four kids. Cole and Tatum were still young enough to believe the gifts came from Santa and not their big sister.

When we opened them, our house was empty of the one person who made those Christmas mornings so special, and your absence ached and ate away at my insides.

I gifted Dad a big frame, holding pictures of the two of you through your shared seventeen years, and he choked back tears, unable to look at them. It was devastating and confusing, and I remember wondering if I should've felt ashamed or accomplished for creating a present that made my unbreakable father cry.

I don't know how he handled it, how he sat down there and watched his kids lose the magic of Christmas, as all the love we once shared seemed to shrivel and shrink and separate into individual hurting hearts.

In the years to come, I want my children to not receive seventy-two presents, but rather a reasonable number they can appreciate. I want them to understand that our family being together, all under the same roof, is what's to be celebrated. And sledding and cookie baking and classic movie watching, all done as a family, is what's to be treasured and remembered—that's what it was always about for you, underneath the fancy parties, underneath our absurd amount of presents.

I don't mean to sound like a sad humbug. Because I really am looking forward to this month of December. Kati is coming home from Texas, Allison turns 24, Yoga Flow is having a holiday party, and we have started seriously trying for baby number two.

With doubt and hesitation stopping the "trying process" for months now, I finally know it's time. It's safe to say Chris has a good few months ahead of him. And at least making-out isn't a requirement to make a baby, because still, I have yet to heal and cannot kiss him.

But when I keep my perspective right, I know realistically that Chris and I are probably happier than a lot of other couples who can press their lips together. And even though at times I feel incredibly self-conscious at the appearance of my lips, that man loves me in a constant manner, in any condition.

Because of him, I truly understand what it means *to love unconditionally*.

I get cross with him when he needs a haircut or if he trimmed his sideburns crooked. But never once, has he ever looked at me even a hint differently, since this whole lip thing started.

Not much is new in the world of Everett. Each morning, he gets up around 6 a.m. and we go downstairs to watch cartoons for an hour or so. It's our lazy time together, when I make breakfast and wake up the house, starting laundry and getting my coveted cup of coffee.

After TV we go upstairs, and Everett sits in his room and flips through hardback books while I dry my hair and wrap it in hot rollers. On a "fun" day, I play music, singing in my bathroom that has a straight and full-view to his room.

He likes dancing to oldies and when *Sherrrry...Sherry baby* comes on, he nods his head and shakes his little body, still while reading. It's so cute.

Everett always looks like he's going to burst of joy—never have I met such a happy kid. He feels like my own extra special exception.

After playtime, he takes a nap, I sit with my new habit of meditation, then start writing until he wakes up. Sometimes I get an hour, sometimes even two, but when he's up, I'm a mom again and I close my office door (which is really just our spare bedroom). I never want to get lost between following a personal dream and doing what makes me most happy—mothering. They have to balance and blend and not outweigh the other, otherwise, I'd have to set this book aside.

However, I'm proud to tell you my proposal is finished. It currently consists of over fifty pages, including parts like the books' overview, sample chapters and a market analysis. So I've set aside the time between now and Christmas, to proof and rearrange and edit it over and over, until I feel confident enough to send it out to the list of literary agents I have pinned to my vision board.

So about that meditation I casually mentioned.

I've consistently meditated Monday through Saturday for almost an entire month now. I set my timer for ten minutes, and that's all together one hour per week that I get to sit, breathe, clear my mind, and make space for more good and positivity.

Countless times before, I'd quit the commitment after a few days because it just seemed too simple to be of any benefit. But meditating is now starting to feel necessary, like every person in the world should try it.

The most important thing I have learned in ten years of practicing yoga is breathing. It's not forward bending, not standing on my hands, not even learning how to teach. It's simply the breath.

And breathing is key for meditation. It creates a rhythm, an awareness and the ability to connect with the greater power that gives me the energy to inhale and exhale in the first place.

When I close my eyes and seal my lips and start slowly breathing through my nose, I'm taken to a place in my head that I wish I could always stay. My focus is strong and my thoughts are intentional, rather than covered up by the constant background noise I wish I could just shut up.

And I'll get an idea about somewhere to go, something to write about, someone to call....which all feels right, like something divine is guiding me and the thought that comes.

I can't explain it without sounding strange. I've tried to tell Chris about my "meditating findings" and knew he was keeping his crazy pedometer on stand-by while still trying to be respectful of his wife. At this point, I have totally accepted the fact that I'm always going to be one of those weird people who believes in spirit and energy and signs from the Universe.

However, I know I can tell you without receiving judgement. Because you exist in that powerful, yet calm place I'm learning to become a part of.

I'd say the best side effect from this meditation (so far), is that I'm beginning to feel like I'm a part of life and the energy that makes up this Universe, not a victim to the circumstances or happenings that occur in my experience.

I don't know how sitting and breathing created that change, but it did.

I cannot be connected with a higher power if I'm sad and depressed and stuck in my mind. I cannot receive the magical evidence, like the Blue Jays, if I don't believe there's a higher power at work. And I cannot feel close to you if I believe you've permanently disappeared.

It's all like comparing a closed flower to an open one—the sunshine simply cannot get in.

The only "price" I have to pay in order to stay connected and open, is put myself in the happy, positive and believing mindset that attracts the good stuff. But why does that sometimes feel so hard, even though my life is so wonderful?

Everett and I were at Whole Foods yesterday, and at the checkout line, there was an older woman in front of us, dressed up like she was coming out of a meeting, with a silk scarf squaring her shoulders and a huge diamond ring that shined as she swiped her credit card. She was with her daughter, who had a baby, and for a moment I felt that pitted pang of jealousy, thinking, *Why can't I have my mother like she does?*

I caught the ringed one looking at me funny, probably judging my from-Maine checkered flannel and moccasins, and she had a smart attitude with the cashier, directing which groceries went into what bags like it really mattered. She and her daughter kept bickering at each other, keeping me entertained live while waiting in line.

But instead of letting any of their bad vibes absorb into mine, I understood their gloomy mood had nothing to do with me, and tried to remember that I get to have you in a more special way than merely physical—that you were indeed there with Everett and I.

After they left and I was rung up, my total came to $23.45, the least amount of money I've ever walked into that store paying, but look at the pattern of the numbers.

While walking to our car, I felt like I was gliding on water, a very part of the sunshine and clear sky and my ever-present mother who always seems to have a way of "showing up" when I need her.

I thought about the fact that if I never lost you, I would've remained a closed flower, just like that woman and her daughter, unaware of my connection to the world all around me, comfortable in pettiness and material things, blind to the sunshine because my petals are pulled shut.

Because you cannot be miserable and expect miracles to manifest.

We are energetic creatures in an energetic Universe, where

everything vibrates at certain frequencies. The higher my vibration (the more I appreciate, the happier I am, the better my thoughts), the closer I am to you—the closer I am to the higher power.

When you died, you returned to the energy that created the Universe. You returned to the energy we all come from, the same energy that grows the grass and shines the sun and moves the wind and gives me my beautiful breath.

As a living human being, I am an extension of that Source Energy, and when my time comes to move into the non-physical, I will return to the Source, just as you did.

So there is always a connection. We are all the same stuff, tethered tightly to all things and always able to reach each other (if we would only stop whining about our lives and choose to feel good).

I feel guilty that it took your death for me to realize what now feels like the foundation of my life. I will not waste this gift you've given me, better than any of the hundreds of Christmas presents I gathered throughout childhood.

And how wonderful it is, to think that my children will grow up, never having to fear losing their parents or anyone else they'll ever love, because in all my power, I will teach them that there is no such thing as separation in our Universe—that severance is only of the mind.

JANUARY 15, 2018

twenty-one months

Seeing is believing, but sometimes the most real things in the world are things we can't see.

-Chris Van Allsburg, *The Polar Express*

First post of the new year, long overdue.

Since we last talked, I've thought about quitting this book, I've thought about starting it over. I've thought about switching my direction entirely, and I've thought about waiting until a "better time" to try and become an author.

Without even realizing it, I started sabotaging myself and the idea of publishing this journal, thinking, *I'll still write a book, just not this one.*

I can now recognize those words as nothing but fear, hiding in disguise and sneaking into my mind like a slithering snake, trying its best to scare me to quits.

But it's intimidating to have two years of work, written out on paper and summarized into one proposal, which gets sent out to huge publishers that probably don't even open my e-mail inquiry.

I have to keep reminding myself:

This project will become all I know it can be.

Because without belief and the certainty that these words will become bound in a book, it's just not possible.

I continually forget that I'm not supposed to know how to do any of this. I'm not supposed to know which publisher is right, which wording is perfect, or how to build my audience. I'm supposed to trust and relax, trust and relax. I'm supposed to keep meditating each morning so I can get my brain quiet enough for the day ahead, ready to hear and see and become aware of all the ways Source is communicating to me the way forward.

And then when I *feel* it, sit down during Everett's nap, and write to you.

So that is my focus now: trust and relax. It sounds like the easiest thing in the world, but yet nothing has proven to be more difficult.

Everett is still happy and fun and literally growing curls out of his ears. Terri recently gave him his first haircut (well, trim). He snacked on cheddar chips the entire time, clueless to the scissors snipping around his forehead. And I kept a curl because every woman who heard about his first haircut, basically demanded that I keep a lock. I dared not to disobey, so it's now in a Ziplock bag in my memory box, waiting to become a small, evidential charm of his childhood.

He's using a spoon to eat yogurt and a fork to prick his apple chicken sausage (the only meat he will eat). The "feed myself process" makes a mess, but I can cook a meal in the kitchen while he's scooping and poking away, examining the bites that make it to his mouth, as well as the pieces that fall onto the floor and become Clifford snacks.

While I teach yoga on Sunday mornings, Chris has been taking Everett to my in-laws, and that way his mother can be with the baby. That's our focus right now: Everett getting as much time with his "Nonni" as he can, because time is still of the limit these days—the clock in her brain refuses to tell us its plans for entirely robbing her memory.

It's getting more difficult to know that my son will most likely, not grow up with her. When he's old enough to understand and she's far along enough in her disease to forget, how do I explain to Everett why his Nonni doesn't know his name?

As much as we never talk about the inevitable ending of Alzheimer's, when she does transition from this world, it will be my duty to teach my children she is always with us, even though their little physical eyes can no longer perceive her—in the same way I've already promised to do for you.

A few days ago, I watched a home video of you, and hours later, while driving in my car alone, I kept crying over and over, each time I remembered the way your face looked, the way your voice sounded, the way we were all permanently recorded together in that special house as a family.

It's been awhile since I've been upset about you, but I don't say that to brag. I say that because I've honestly forgotten that you used to be a physical person. I have become so used to thinking of you as unseen energy, like my little personal spirit, that when I saw you on video, you came alive again and I felt my heart flutter and pound and silently whisper over and over, *mom mom mom mom.*

I felt like I was your tiny baby again, needing the one person who felt natural and right to take care of me.

But in that grief, in that sadness, I have learned that just because I can't see you, doesn't mean you're not real, which is perhaps one of the strangest lessons for us humans to learn.

It makes me think of the Polar Express book Nana would always read to us kids at Christmas. At the end, she'd gently shake the jingle-less bell, saying that only those who believed would hear its ring. We'd all say, "I hear it! I hear it!" after it was individually held up to each of our ears.

I can feel more than anything, how much I want Everett and all our future children, to never stop believing in that magic. Because we all come into this world with that sense of mystery, but lose it when everyone else around us starts questioning it, trying to come up with answers, like as to why Santa Clause can't come down a chimney.

But that's why I have to keep writing. How can I look at my kids and tell them all these beautiful truths I'm learning to remember, if right now, at this pivotal "becoming era" I feel like I'm in, I shrink back into myself, afraid of failure and surrendering to doubt? It just wouldn't work.

It seems I need to keep reminding myself to continue believing in my capability, each and every time I go on a binge of self-doubt. It seems I have to keep reminding myself that you're still real.

But I don't want to feel ashamed of those things anymore, thinking, *Why can't I just get this stuff right once and for all?* Because I'm not supposed to.

And I want anyone who ever reads these words to remember that it's okay if they have to keep reminding themselves that they're beautiful, that they're powerful, that they're capable.

Because I think that's a part of our physical journey: to constantly keep remembering to believe in all the good—to *consciously choose* to believe in the good...about ourselves, about each other and the world around us. Because the magic is always there, hidden in plain sight, for anyone who wants to search for it.

JANUARY 25, 2018

You are never alone or helpless. The force that guides the stars guides you too.

-Prabhat Ranjan Sarkar

I don't have much time to write, but I've had the feeling I'm pregnant. Our past two "tries," I thought the same thing, but I feel like I did before finding out I was carrying Everett—I'm not questioning it, I honestly and truly feel that I am, for reasons I can't explain.

Last night I decided to pull a tarot card (Chris sometimes likes to play the game with me at night before bed, to my absolute surprise) and I got the queen of hearts. She had long flowing hair and green eyes and was holding with her hands, centered at her chest, a bowl overflowing with flowers and fruit and I said to him, "I bet this means a baby."

She looked literally fruitful and motherly and like the beautiful goddess I try to convince myself I really am. Pulling that card was the intuitive proof I needed for the way I'd been feeling. And coincidentally (or not), hearts in the tarot deck represents your intuition and emotions.

Hoping to prove Chris' doubts otherwise about my gypsy cards, I looked up in my little guidebook what the queen stood for:

Fertility.

I bet my lucky stars I'm carrying our second child.

I won't ever have actual "evidence" that that queen of hearts card was meant to be pulled, right on the day that I kept thinking on and off: *I'm pregnant. No I'm not. Yes I am! Nope, no you're not.* But the way I felt when I read it—it solidified everything.

All wrapped up into one teensy moment, I felt you, I felt assured, I felt a part of a great power, I felt taken care of and most importantly, heard and answered.

May I trust beautiful moments like this one, knowing each and every time, that everything is always, without exception, working out for me with perfect timing. That I truly am guided by the same force of the stars.

We all are.

FEBRUARY 2, 2018

twenty-two months + six weeks

All around you are spirits, child. They live in the earth, the water, the sky. If you listen, they will guide you.

-Grandmother Willow

Life with Everett continues to color our days here at home with fun, laughs, and the perfect amount of frustration. He's discovering how to climb and be cleverly mischievous, sneaking his little hands into everything possible.

I'm learning the balance of when to yell and when to calmly correct him. When he doesn't listen, sometimes raising my voice works, but most of the time I just scare him and then feel terrible. And it makes me upset and worked up. But it's so easy to scream. I feel like you when I do it.

A small part of me likes that, like *yes be tough like mom was.* And then another part—the softer part, nudges a reminder: that's not you and you don't have to do everything just like her.

What can I say—I'm learning.

When we took a walk a few days ago, he wanted to stop and play in the grass. After waiting there too long, I told him to *let's go!* but he wouldn't budge. I even tried walking away but he could've cared less. So I dragged him by his arm for a few forceful steps until he laid practically face down on the pavement in a temper tantrum. I forced him to stand and got him to walk by singing a song about what a big boy he was.

You're a walking boy, yes yes yes, going home to see your bunny and eat snacks!

Singing silly felt like a win. Dragging him and yelling did not. But who knows what type of mother I'll be when more kids come along.

Recently I moved my bunny upstairs because he's been stationed in the dark basement all day, seeing or hearing no signs of life. And it's obviously too cold to return outside in his hutch. So now he's around all of us, and Everett likes to blow him kisses and throw pieces of his leftover lunch through the cage. Yesterday it was potato latkes. Everett can't leave the bunny alone, but I don't blame him. It's cute to see him love his animals so much.

I feel like I'm ready to burst through the walls of our house though, wanting warmer air and the ability to go outside for regular walks and playtime. It's nice getting to relax, watch movies and eat— that's honestly what our days revolve around now, but cabin fever is a real term for a stay at home mom in wintertime.

We are going out to eat tonight as a family and I've been thinking about it all week, like it's the outing of a lifetime, because I get to leave the house for reasons other than Target or Trader Joe's.

Everett's favorite movie right now is Hercules. We've watched it too many times to count. I put it on for him the other day and actually snuck a shower in while he was cuddled on the couch with a blanket, sippy cup, and Clifford. I felt like an accomplished superwoman.

He also likes Pocahontas, and spins and sings when the Native Americans do their chants around the fire. I know it's a feminine movie, but I grew up watching all those classics, each having an important lesson. When she runs through the woods and sings about the rivers and the animals being her brothers, and that *we are all connected to each other, in a circle that never ends*, I repeat the stuck-in-my-head lyrics while wiping down the kitchen counter, feeling dumb, but remembering that you are never far, because even Pocahontas says so.

I recently stopped the early 6 a.m. yoga class I taught on Wednesdays. Chris is going back to school for his masters and cannot go into work late anymore while he watches Everett. So I will now have one class, on Sunday mornings, and something about that just feels right. It gives me more opportunity to practice on my own mat during the week, and it's one less day of getting up hours before the sun.

And it's great timing, because I am in fact pregnant.

This second time around already feels so different than with Everett. When I found out I was pregnant with him, the thought of pregnancy filled every mental second. I immediately read blogs and articles and books, and was so excited to learn as much as I could about what was happening inside my body and what life would be like once the baby was out.

I still get all gooey every time I tell someone the new news, but keep forgetting about those two pink positive lines on my test. I remember when I want to have a beer and think, *Nope can't do that for a while.* Or when I wonder why I've been so tired in the afternoons or why my mood is for once stable.

The pausing of my menstrual cycle is the best thing about being pregnant. Hormones are whacky while growing a human, but for me personally, it doesn't compare to the ups and downs I feel during my moon cycle.

What's a moon cycle? I can already hear you asking.

I've been reading a lot about the moon and its connection to women's menstrual cycles, trying in any way to understand why I've always been so influenced by my period. Because no one really talks about them. And you certainly never did. The only thing you ever told me about puberty was that you grow boobs.

We were at one of my horse-riding lessons and my teacher joked, saying something like, "Oh you just wait until you hit puberty." Not knowing what that word meant, I later asked and you gave that one simple answer. I think back then it wasn't as normal to talk about our bodies as it is today.

My menstrual cycle has had so much control over me, I tried anti-depressants when Everett was nine months old—remember? I didn't know what else to do and figured since you'd been on that same medication before during certain times in your life, it was okay for me to be, too.

But after a month, I stopped, knowing I had control over my body and was determined to learn about the power of being positive. It seemed like my only choice. And thus my journey of understanding the Universe and thoughts and appreciation and all that stuff I bore you with was started.

Between when my period starts and ovulation, I'm at my emotional best. This is my "highest highs" phase, when I sing in the car, believe I can write, and feel beautiful in my skin. I'm expressive, happy, have enthusiasm and new ideas—everything just feels good and balanced.

That lasts for about fourteen days and then comes ovulation. This is where the luteal phase begins, a phase I hated for all my teenage years and young adult life. Ever since I started my cycle, I never understood why I felt so different for half of the month. I didn't understand why I felt emotional about everything, why I questioned my decisions, etc. This was always when I missed you the most, the times I'd lay in bed buried under the covers and cry until there was nothing left to empty out.

I'd judge myself and feel lazy and unproductive. My body would bloom a little fuller, especially in my chest and belly, and every month, I always thought I was just getting "fat." So I'd eat less and exercise more, doing exactly the opposite of what my body needed most: rest and nourishment. For half of the month, I hated my body and how it made me feel. If I would indulge into my natural cravings, I'd throw the food right up.

A lot of past problems stemmed from not understanding my body.

But during the luteal phase, instead of hating myself and wondering why I'm crazy, it's my time to reflect and go inward. It's my time for me, to sleep and eat more, journal and stay home—not feel like a piece of shit. This is hard, especially as a mother, but it has forced me to be more kind to myself and not feel selfish for taking a small nap on the days Chris gets home from work early.

In the cycles of nature, there are ebbs and flows within the seasons, the tides, and the waxing/waning of the moon. This mimics the cycle that is within women, the cycle that governs not only the flow of blood, but the flow of creativity and information. It's instinctive and natural and connects us with something greater than ourselves. At least I believe so.

What's amazing about all of this is that the moon phase goes in a circle of 29.5 days, the average length of a woman's menstrual cycle. And the phases of the moon mirror what happens inside our bodies during ovulation. It's even been scientifically proven that during a full moon (representing a ripe and ready egg in our uterus), women are more fertile.

I don't fully understand it all, but that's not the point—I truly believe I'm supposed to feel the highs and lows and work with the monthly cycle within my body, not against it.

These are ideals I want to teach my girls (if I have any, of course—Chris is convinced we'll have all boys). I was educated on periods in middle school, but with the undertone of *ew that's so gross* and *don't ever have sex or you'll get pregnant and die.* There was no connection of the physical body and the emotional moods. And if there ever was, it was somehow all boiled down into the worst combination of three letters: PMS.

I don't need my kids to pretend they're Pocahontas and sleep outside to sync up their periods with the actual moon. But I will explain to them why they feel a little crazy during that luteal phase. I will teach them how to track their cycles, even if they have irregular periods or what not.

Even though you weren't alive by the time I started having sex, I can tell you now that I never relied on birth control. Well condoms, but not medicine. I tried it a few times, hoping it would regulate my moods, but never liked how it made me feel. So I learned to track my cycle, became aware of when I was fertile, and always used protection.

And knowing your rhythms makes getting pregnant a bit easier...

Boo-ya!

I really feel as if I got pregnant at the right time. As my body is creating life within, I can continue to create this writing into a reality. It's a beautiful comparison if you think about it.

Oh and guess what—my best friend is getting married! Jessie is officially engaged, planning for a November wedding.

The baby will be guaranteed out by that time, and I keep picturing myself with my long hair and a baby on my boob, drinking a Blue Moon, set to lips that are finally tinted with my "Ruby Woo" colored lipstick, on my best friend's big day.

Talk about goals.

Thank you for where I am. Thank you for the timing of my life. Thank you for the sudden clarity I feel in my mind, as my body begins to take on a new form, creating our second child.

MAY 4, 2018

twenty-five months + nineteen weeks

It was about no longer being the kind of person who takes what she can get, and finally becoming the kind of person who creates exactly what she wants.

-Jen Sincero

When I wrote the below goals in my pen and paper journal a little over a year ago, I created a direction to drive my determination and follow through with a visual plan to write this book:

post to blog every two weeks

40 posts total

roughly 1,500 words each

100 minimum pages total of book

written proposal for agents

submit queries by April 2018

I'm proud to tell you that I did each of those bullet points, even the last one: I've been submitting query letters (whose purpose is to convince an agent to request your proposal) since January, and even heard back from one. Even though it was a kind decline, I got an agent (in London, no less!) to read my "application," which in the literary world, I'm taking as a small accomplishment.

But during my silent months of March and April, of which have now created a gap in this journal, I wrote to you several times and just felt flat, like there was nothing flowing through me, and had nothing of importance to tell you. So I'd occasionally accept the idea of stopping this project (yet again). I was even beginning to feel content with that decision.

Usually an entry just spits out through the keyboard in one sitting. And then I'll re-read and edit and proof over and over, until I feel it's worthy of people like Nana or friends on Facebook, to read and possibly relate.

I don't know if I can blame this productivity drop on pregnancy, but I can say that these past months have proven more difficult than while pregnant with Everett. I'm fine physically, and with the beginning spouts of morning sickness having surpassed (like nausea, wanting to vomit when I saw green vegetables, eating frozen pizza for breakfast), I thought I'd be back into feeling all vibrant without my monthly cycles. Because that's at least how it worked with Everett.

At my first prenatal appointment with the midwives, they asked the routine question of how I'd been feeling. And I couldn't fake my response. I said, "Fine!" in that stupid, too high-pitched tone, knowing the expression on my face was probably silently pleading, *help me.*

I explained how I infamously have trouble before my menstrual cycle, and the midwife looked right at me and sweetly said, "Since pregnancy is basically like one big luteal phase, how do you do while pregnant?" And I thought, *Damn that luteal phase! Always getting me.*

She suggested I see their on-site therapist when I come in every 4-6 weeks for the routine appointments, and I agreed, figuring it couldn't hurt, and that it's probably a good idea to stay on top of the whole depression question that's been dangling in my mind.

A few weeks later, I was in the therapist's office, listening to her talk with one ear and one eye, while watching Everett with the other observing set. He was touching everything from her coffee mug, to yoga blocks and business cards, all while eating a messy peanut butter and jelly sandwich, intermittently watching his favorite show "Tumble Leaf" on my iPhone.

And while I instantly knew this therapist wasn't "the one" for me, I didn't want to miss the opportunity for some kind of help. So I later made the decision to call my previous therapist from my "after college era."

She truly helped me save myself, in a time when I needed to decide if I was going to follow what was expected of me (continue with more school and/or start a career), or if I was going to keep supporting myself with teaching yoga and babysitting, in the hopes that I'd soon be a stay at home mom, with no debt or career to leave behind.

And she helped me know Chris was the man I was supposed to marry, something I'd known for years and years, but got scared to officially accept, because it meant closing a secret, coveted corner of my heart, even though I still loved its past inhabitant. It meant acknowledging I wouldn't share my life with someone you once knew. It meant feeling defeated or wronged that Mrs. Treml wouldn't be my mother-in-law, even though at times throughout my youth, I honestly pictured her holding my imaginary children.

I wanted it to be "him" because he was the one that would come to the old house after school in ninth grade, and sit at the kitchen island, having coffee and your homemade pumpkin pie, talking with you and I. And then years later, knelt with me at your casket, holding me as I said over and over, *What am I going to do? What am*

I going to do?

He was the only other person I ever loved. And he *knew you.* But because of this, it took me way too many years to realize he wasn't the type for a stubborn, demanding flower as I—and that I didn't have to hold on to what never held onto me.

I feel somewhat ashamed for anonymously mentioning him yet again in this journal, but he has always been a part of me, and I cannot ignore what my heart wants to say.

Anyways. I saw my therapist last week, and I'm glad I did. It felt good and appropriate to catch-up, explaining how different this pregnancy feels, how I keep forgetting about it and then wondering if that's normal, and how stuck I feel, creating a baby in the midst of miserable hormones, uninspired to keep writing to you.

Talking in a comfortable environment allowed me to empty out the many tangled questions and fears, coincidentally preparing me for a great planned weekend away without Chris or Everett.

The next morning, Nana came around ten o'clock to watch Everett, so I could hit the road towards Annapolis, Maryland, to my girlfriend Olivia's apartment. I was staying for a visit and the *You Are a Badass* book signing in Baltimore. I wasn't again going to miss a chance to meet my girl crush.

The entire car ride there, I kept seeing signs that made me feel like I was going towards something exciting—something that was going to help lift my spirits. I'd pass the 1111.1 mile marker, happening to catch its glance in a split second. Or I saw a big motor vehicle with the logo "Puma" painted across the side, which has been Chris' nickname for me since the beginning.

Once I arrived and settled in, Olivia and I went into the city for a delicious Thai dinner, and then walked into the John Hopkins campus store to get a coffee at Starbucks. Apparently the University's mascot is my special Blue Jay, which were displayed everywhere on t-shirts, mugs, posters, etc. I knew I was in the right place, like everything was lining up for a fantastic evening.

Our Starbucks total came to $7.53. And when we had left her apartment earlier, Olivia's car dashboard clock said 3:57. It's the same consecutive odd numbers, flipped.

As I've already journaled in previous entries, these are the little things that make life feel exciting—that make me feel like you and I can still connect, and that the timing in my life is always perfect. I get this trusting, reassuring rush, that lights up everything inside me, until I start to doubt it and think it's silly to pay attention to things like numbers and birds and pumas.

We walked across the street to the book signing, located in a cute local bookshop, and found seating. There was the perfect amount of people—not too crowded, but not like no one cared to show up. And books were neatly shelved on all the walls around us, creating a cozy and inspiring environment that I was thankful to be in.

When Jen Sincero walked through the entrance door, I stared and stared like she was the most famous person in the world, not "just" a best-selling author. I was giddy, and Olivia and I kept making little gossip comments like, *She's so tall! I love her shirt. Oh my God.*

Hearing her speak in person took everything I ever read and blew it up into big-sized pieces, ones that I was eating by the mouthful, while my inner voice was simultaneously saying, *You can do this...you can do this...you will write your book!* I could feel how sure I was, that being published could and would be done.

It felt like the energetic boost I'd been needing lately.

She was telling her story about being broke and wanting so desperately to be rich and "stop sucking," and explained how excruciating it felt to know you're not living up to your true potential. And for me, hearing that was like *ding ding ding!*

That's what has hurt the most during these last few months: the knowing of how wonderful this book could be, if I only believed and continued to believe in it and myself.

I would keep making excuses to stop writing, as I have in the past, but these ones felt truly legitimate. I told myself that I've accomplished my dream already, of being a mom and having a happy home and family. Which is entirely true. But it's not complete.

In the back of my (now signed!) copy of *You Are a Badass*, a long long time ago, I wrote in pink permanent pen:

I will have a beautiful home

All of my many children will be healthy

My writing will become something meaningful

I will always believe in myself and LOVE WHO I AM

And lately in this pregnancy slump, if I settled into the thought that I've already met my goals, I could convince myself of being content. But denying myself the ability to grow, especially when I can see and feel and imagine how good it will feel to rise further towards the sun, has now become more difficult than staying put and settling back down into familiar soil.

By avoiding the pain and fear we're afraid of, we create it and *stay in it*, because moving forward involves too much risk and judgement and unknown and "work."

I seemed to have still been under the impression that I could choose to stay comfortable and just be happy with the beautiful life I have now, even if I never became a writer.

Because I have a great home. I have a healthy child, with one on the way. I am married to my best friend. That's enough, right?

Of course it is. But not when I can feel down into the deepest parts of me, what it will feel like to get published and to start building the house we desire, on the property we dream of, with a plethora of kids and animals.

Like Jen said, it feels excruciating to ignore that inner voice. And until I heard her say that, my inner voice was being squashed with reason and responsibility and perspective and "reality."

The smallest bout of doubt will shatter my desire to move forward, something that has happened over and over again throughout this writing journey. As soon as I get something accomplished, like finishing my proposal, I get comfortable and content with "enoughness," conceiving unlimited reasons why it's time to dust my fingers free and stop tapping the keyboard.

I've submitted query letters—something that last February I was setting as one of my bullet point goals—and then just quit, settling into that *okay I did it, I'm done now,* because continuing on meant more rejection, more belief, more unknown.

I don't know how many more times I'm going to get dragged down by doubt. It may be something I'm always going to fight against, or maybe by the grace of all that is holy, this shift is permanent.

I even almost persuaded myself to not drive to Maryland. That voice was saying, *You don't have to leave and drive four hours, when's the last time you even drove that far by yourself?*

Me, getting scared to drive to another state. This is the girl who once took trains and boats around Amsterdam alone, almost too merrily stoned and not an ounce less scared, to read the transporting tickets that would get her safely back to her abroad home in London.

One last thing I want to share with you.

While driving to Maryland, I was listening to a recorded Esther Hicks seminar. You may not remember, but this is the woman who channels a spirit and speaks about energy and attraction and thought—all that fun stuff I love telling you about, and her books and lectures still teach me an incredible amount since I found them last January.

But as I navigated the highway, trying safely to hear the GPS and good ol' Esther, I happened to catch her say: *Anytime you feel negative emotion, it's because you're going against the person you're becoming.*

It was another *ding ding ding!*

We are all constantly becoming, a very part of this beautiful forward flow of energy that creates the world around us. And when we go against the current, when we deny that inner voice inside and stay safe, choosing a career because our parents say so, or wussing and excusing ourselves out of a needed weekend away from family, it hurts. It muddles our light and we feel terrible, stuck in the trying circle of convincing ourselves it was the right choice...it was the smart choice...I didn't need to go anyways, etc.

I don't want to go against who I'm becoming anymore. I don't want to be afraid. I don't want to be a wimp. I don't want to stay put. I don't want to settle in familiarity, even though I am a creature that thrives on comfort and things staying the same.

Because I can't. It's come to hurt too much, like I'm going to burst if I don't naturally allow myself to turn towards the sun and grow.

And my true eventual hope is that someday, somebody will read this journal of my becoming, knowing that they can grow in the light, too.

MAY 25, 2018

The female being has been chosen by the creator to be the portal between the spiritual realm and the physical realm; the only force on Earth powerful enough to navigate unborn spirits onto this planet.

-Unknown

Everett is now almost two months past the two year mark. He's becoming a little boy right in front of my eyes, suddenly seeming giant in his stroller, high chair, crib, and car seat.

Ever since his birthday, I've noticed something different each day that propels him forward into mini boyhood—a new word, a new mannerism, a new understanding. A part of me feels proud that I've guided him this far, yet another cannot believe he was once the little baby I'd swaddle and rock and hold close to my chest.

Which speaking of babies, I'm finally starting to anticipate this second addition's arrival.

We had the 20-week anatomy sonogram last week.

While Chris chased Everett around the room saying *no* fifteen times over, I stared at the little black and white projection screen, lost in wonderment, as the technician whirled around my jellied belly, looking for the makings of a healthy baby.

She checked the chambers of the heart and took measurements of little details, like the baby's head shape, the umbilical cord, and the size of its thumbs.

It was so temping to find out the sex. The technician said she was able to tell, and I couldn't believe she held that information in her head—she knew if Everett would be growing up with a brother or sister!

But I don't feel ready to know yet. I truly like keeping it a surprise, and especially love seeing everyone's reaction when Chris and I say we don't know if it's a boy or girl. Most people are shocked and then almost all reply with, "Well, there are few true surprises in life!"

When I think about packing two different colored outfits in my hospital bag, I feel giddy. I'm so excited that I'm pregnant. I'm so excited that we are growing our family, and I'm absolutely thrilled that this time I'll have the hospital experience, getting to sit in bed while my family and friends meet the new life I just brought into the world.

After Everett was born and immediately transferred to the hospital with Chris, I had to stay at The Midwife Center for a span of time that I honestly can't recount because it's been blocked from my memory. What I do remember is when Chris came back for me, I simply sat up from the bed, my pants stuffed with pads and icepacks, and walked down the hallway, out of the center, passing the nurse's room on my out and casually saying, "Bye! Thanks!"

They panicked and all looked like they were going to communally hurl, telling me I had papers to fill out and information to hear before being discharged. All I wanted was to hold Everett, and the thought of that initial separation isn't something I ever think about, but right now, it's making my eyes cry.

How frightening that must've all been.

But I feel brave when it comes to this birth because I know separation cannot happen like it did prior, at least not from different facilities. I know I'll get to stay in one place. I know Chris will remain with me. And I think I want Allison there when I deliver.

She and Chris have developed a brother sister relationship, something that makes me love my husband even more. He consistently calls her Saus (her family nickname) and asks every Saturday if she wants to come over for our Green Mango takeout night. And Allison can freely squeeze out his solid and practical advice about things such as credit card scores and how a man should treat her.

It's special to see your spouse and siblings together. She won't only be my support at the birth, but Chris' too, as funny as that may sound.

But I still have a ways to go until all of that, so I won't say anymore—but it does feel good to be looking forward to the near future, a very different mindset from where I was a few months ago. The second trimester of pregnancy really is the best, both physically and mentally.

As I said, Everett is growing at a pace I cannot keep up with. He is a true 4T in all clothes, and his stalky build allows him to plow and push through anything. Chris' Aunt Nancy calls him Tank, for good reason. He's not overweight in the slightest, just as solid as could be.

At his two year check-up, he measured 90% for both height and weight and my past inner cheerleader silently shouted, *That's my boy!*

He plays outside in our yard all day long. There aren't many toys out there, but he finds sticks and little garden shovels and entertains himself in hidden rain puddles and piles of dirt. Sometimes he'll come inside with mulch stuffed inside a back pocket, zippered up as if he's saving it for later.

When Everett makes up his mind and doesn't get his way, he still throws theatrical fits, as I'm sure most toddlers do. Usually I'll bend down to his level, turn his shoulders towards me and say, "Look at Mommy." His sad eyes will immediately come to match mine, waiting for my words to reassure or fix the situation.

I'll say things like, "It's okay, we just have to stay inside because it's raining. Do you have to go nunnies?"

In which he'll reply with a very loud and long *nooooo!* And that little threat of sleep almost always makes him stop a fit. If it doesn't, then I ignore him and trust the anger will run out of his system naturally.

I don't know if either of these are "good" parenting tactics, but they work in this household. The other alternative is to yell, and when I join in on his big display of emotion, it only makes for two tantrums.

I'm definitely not a mushy parent. There is a time to yell. There is almost always a time to lose your shit. But as I'm continually trying to be aware of my emotions and how I'm feeling energetically, I don't wish to step off the line of balance that I work really hard to achieve, just to yell at him for painting his face with vanilla yogurt.

Before a nap and before bedtime, he insists on reading The Lorax. I catch myself throughout the day reciting lines, saying in my head:

Mister!" he said with a sawdusty sneeze...

I am the Lorax, I speak for the trees!

I speak for the trees for the trees have no tongues,

And I'm asking you sir, at the top of my lungs...

What's that THING you've made out of my truffula tuft?

Sometimes in the car, I'll say this memorized phrase in my funny reading voice, and glance back at Everett (sitting forward in his car seat now like a big boy!), who is gleaming, balling his hands together by his smiling cheeks, like his Mom and the Lorax are both just too cool to handle.

I love the person I am through his eyes.

He eats a packet of oatmeal each and every morning, and I swear 95% of his mass is made up of oats. He loves it. After he's done, he hands me his bowl, I take him out of his chair, and he runs over to the couch, waiting for me to put on a movie.

Recently though, this small window of movie time has been forgotten about; he'd rather get right outside.

And whether he's on the couch or frolicking in the backyard, I make my breakfast. It's twenty or so minutes that I cherish, a time that I get to myself to mentally start out right for the day.

Sometimes I'll catch myself cursing that I broke my egg yoke, and then feeling pissy when I eat it, which is absurd. And that momentum can easily pick up, when for example, I go upstairs to brush my teeth afterwards, and Everett follows me, opening up the vanity cupboard and spilling out each individual hot hair roller from its resting peg.

I'll get flustered, frustrated, and before learning the power of awareness, I wouldn't know how to separate myself from those emotions, so I'd absorb them, allowing the fellow feelings of worry and anger to follow me around and join the mental party.

Worrying is using your imagination to create something you don't want.

When I realize I'm circling scenarios around in my head, trying to reach for an invisible answer, I simply stop, knowing I cannot benefit from it, and then try to think of something else. The trick is catching myself—of becoming *aware* of when I'm within that negative momentum.

Remember in the last entry I talked about that natural forward flowing stream? Well worrying is moving upstream. And the more time I've been spending floating down river, with the understanding that I can't control much, just the way I feel (and therefore the energy I'm sending out/what energy comes back to me), working upstream feels so incredibly hard and nothing but a waste of time.

I can't stress enough how much everyone would benefit from sitting and breathing and observing and checking in with themselves and their higher power, even for just five minutes a day. It's something I wish I could've taught you when you were still alive.

And with this consistent meditation, comes strengthening your intuition, which has become my new personal pal. With a clear mind, I can sometimes hear it, not just feel it. And it'll say, *grab this book, call this person, get this coffee*, creating coincidences throughout my day that prove a higher power is real, somehow magically master-minding the evidence.

At times, this "proof" makes me question how I'm not always in a state of awe, to be a literal part of the beauty and brains that is the Universe. When people complain about insignificant things, when they beep their horns one too many times and flick me off for not changing lanes fast enough, or whatever it is—I feel sorry there are humans so consumed in matters of no consequence.

I saw a picture of you the other day, a blown up black and white one that Nana captured while you were holding Tatum as a baby. And I just stared at it, almost shocked for a second, because I hadn't seen your pictured face for so long.

It feels like such a dream to imagine you living again—my brain just sometimes remembers the years that you were still alive as "too good to be true."

But as I kept staring, I could feel my body warmly respond to your face and all I could think was, *I am my mother's daughter. I am this woman's child. She was my mother. She IS my mother.*

So from now on, when I catch myself feeling overwhelmed or sad or whatever the situation may be that's trying to rock me off this preferred center, I want to try and remind myself of whose child I am—that I am not alone, that I was not just dropped off on Earth.

Because I once belonged in you, just as my sweet star of an unborn baby now belongs in me.

P.S.- the baby is due October 2nd, Mrs. Treml's birthday.

JULY 9, 2018

twenty-seven months + twenty-eight weeks

The moth and the fish eggs are in their place,
The suns I see and the suns I cannot see are all in their
place,
The palpable is in its place and the impalpable is in its
place.

-Walt Whitman, *Leaves of Grass*

The third trimester has officially begun.

I've reasoned that with the time remaining, there are only twelve more Monday mornings for Everett and I to go Trader Joe's, as just the two of us.

I don't know what it is about the grocery store, but we both love going. I enjoy meal planning and then the crossing off of items on my list, while I gather ingredients and snacks and the $3.99 fresh-cut bundled flowers that brighten my bedroom each week.

Everett happily sits in the cart and says *hi* to a few of the workers that he recognizes from being a frequent shopper. Sometimes I'll pack him a peanut butter and jelly sandwich to eat while we stroll around the store, or he'll eat a banana and an oatmeal bar right off the shelf.

And when we pay for the empty wrapper and peel at checkout, he tries handing each of our items to the cashier, saying, "Here ya go!" in a too loud of tone, but it's annoyingly cute.

I imagine simple errands will soon become more of a hassle and involve an increased amount of frustration with another child...I imagine a lot of things are going to change with this second addition. But the becoming part is over now—I am already a mother, and Chris is already a father.

For those reasons, I feel both thankful and prepared as I possibly could be.

Tatum finds it funny that Chris was once just a dude in high school, who wore flat baseball caps and thought it was cool having his initials tattooed to his arm. When she giggles and says, *He's just such a Dad now!* I feel proud, because even someone as young as her, can so obviously tell how much he loves being Everett's father.

It seems he and I have really found the true purpose within our marriage—being parents. While raising our son together, we've unintentionally sifted into the best version of ourselves.

The two of us often casually talk about whether or not to wait in between the next (two) kids. He teased me the other day and said, "Do you really think you want four of these?" while pointing at Everett, who was screaming on the floor in a bedtime protest.

I told him we are too good of parents not to have that many. And added, "You know that the family we form is all we'll really have."

Because he and I both know what it's like to have a mother

who is sick. We both know the changes it creates within a family; how vacations become scarce and then disappear, how dinners out together become rare, and how each member handles grief and acceptance in varying ways.

You were our family's sun. We all orbited around you, like little planets that had their own individual needs and characteristics, thriving off your warmth and light and directional pull.

When we lost the center to this virtual solar system, we stopped circling in the same direction and began again on different planes.

Dad's took him somewhere far away, where parts of him I think were forever lost. I fought blindly to get back to you. Allison and Cole both traveled forward in a kind of silence. And Tatum, being the youngest, was frozen in space, only held up by the gravity of others who loved her.

But I am now that contagious light for Chris, Everett, this baby, and all our children yet to be.

That's why I want such a big family. That's why four kids sounds right when my husband and I talk about it...not because you had that many, but because I want my light to provide all the life and nourishment and guidance that it possibly can.

It's because becoming my own mother sun, is what ultimately allowed me to heal after your death.

Chris and I recently came very close to purchasing some land. That sounds like an incredibly insane statement, because even though I've always believed in our property, I also understood that the finding and financing would be years and years away. But it almost happened.

A few Saturday nights ago, we were on the couch eating our usual Thai takeout, watching a rented movie. During a quick break to wash my face and ritually light the bathroom candles, Chris had scrolled through his phone and found a new property listing online. We were intrigued by the price and location, but unable to tell what it really looked like through the realtor's pictures.

Immediately filling with excitement, we agreed to go see it. It was past 8 p.m. and Everett was already hours into his night sleep, but we woke him up, brought him and his blankets and the dog to the car, and made the drive to the property.

Everett followed the moon for the entire car ride. He'd point when it would pop through the clouds and say *uh-oh* when it disappeared again.

The land was mostly on a slope, had a small leveled part, and then went uphill again. We quickly figured out that that's why it was priced so low.

But we went back the next day, because by then it was getting too dark and too late to try and hike the hills. Chris wore Everett in the backpack, and together, we walked the whole way to the top, curious to see what was at the peak.

It turns out there was a flat wooded acre, sitting at one of the highest points in the town we both grew up in. And the entire background of this property was a nature reserve, a place for our planned clan of children to thrive, where no one else could ever build.

I felt incredible up there. You couldn't hear the far away road, just the birds and the wind and whatever sound describes that kind of natural quiet.

So we contacted a realtor. We contacted the water authority. We contacted a plumber. We contacted the local building inspector. We figured out ways we could finance and what was involved for payment on land.

It wasn't a straight forward picture, since where we'd ideally build a house (in future years to come) was all the way at the top of two hills. Water would need pumped up there, we'd need a sewage system, and have to swallow the cost of propane for our power source.

But still, we continued to visit the land, bringing Everett each time, who would touch the bark on trees we passed, or spy butterflies flying around the plentiful wild flowers. We'd measure and plot and explore. I'd look at my vision board each night, amazed at how closely I could picture the house I've envisioned for so long, sitting on that land.

Before making an offer, we needed to figure out how to get a driveway uphill. We had a local guy come look at the land, and he basically scoffed, saying it was impossible. Then we had an excavating company do the same thing. And finally, just to be sure, we had an engineer do the math, calculating the legal slope limit and how many curves would be required to make it to the flat acre on top.

Again, it was another no. This man at least said it could be done, but Chris and I obviously don't want a scary and dangerous driveway attached to our forever home.

While I feel disappointed, I'm holding onto the feeling of that land. The way we felt up there, the way we felt when we talked about it through last week's dinner conversations—it tells me something was special. Something connected, and even though that may not be the place we end up settling on, it opened our eyes to the fact that our dreams of owning land may not be as far off as we think.

And I know it all made Chris equally excited about having a large family, where we'd be secluded on our own little homestead. He shares my same vision.

I feel relaxed about it. I honestly trust that our plot is out there, waiting for us. I know as confidently as I can, that the Universe will provide it, without the need for worry or rushing.

This is probably how I'm supposed to feel about all of my desires— how we're all supposed to feel about the things we want in life. And that everything is where its meant to be, waiting to come into fruition under the perfect timing that runs this round globe through space.

For reasons I can finally trust without fully understanding, you are in your proper place, too, even if I can't kiss you or hug you or hear the voice I've known since safely inhabiting your womb.

And even if you've become what Walt Whitman would describe as impalpable: *unable to be felt by touch, not easily comprehended, incapable of being perceived by the senses*, you are still in your place.

If I continually accept that what's gone is only the physical part of you, I'm free.

You are much more than skin, bone and heart.

You are my mothering sun, the nourishing light I will always grow towards.

AUGUST 4, 2018
twenty-eight months + thirty-two weeks

If a Blue Jay shows up it means:
Whatever the situation that has triggered some fear, attack it boldly and courageously. Assess your main gifts and talents, develop a plan as to how you can best use them, and then take clear and purposeful action. Choose the project you've started and finish it.

-Dr. Steven D. Farmer, *Animal Spirit Guides*

It's hard to describe the feeling I get, when I so desperately want you here and real, not as a thought inside my mind or unseen energy. It sometimes seems the answer to bringing you back is so obvious, but for the life of me, I can't seem to figure it out...

Like if I could just project myself far enough up into the clouds, I could burst through the Universe and somehow find where you've been hiding all this time. Or like there was truly a way to collect your scattered pieces and place them together, so I could hug and hold and hear you once again.

But I have to shake these fantasies quickly, because they make me feel utterly unworthy, incapable of reeling you back into this realm.

In reality, I know it's absolutely beyond my control and more importantly, there is no "you," sitting somewhere with your leather high heels and leopard pants, waiting for me or anyone else to come find you.

And while I've particularly missed you during the past few weeks, I had an encounter that blew the emotional blues right out of my sappy bones, and replaced them with the reassuring reminder that you really are closer than I could possibly conceive.

Yesterday Everett and I were having a good morning; breakfast was easy, my coffee was strong, the weather had a relieving chill—all the little checks were correctly crossing off, and it put me in an easy state of appreciation.

While on our routine walk, Everett looked back at me from below in his stroller, giving me this cute and contented smile. I could tell in his eyes, he was loving that beautiful morning just as much as his mom.

There have been so many recent and similar times when I've looked at him and simply cannot believe this little human of mine has never met my mother. I cannot believe that he'll grow into a young man who will never quite fully understand, just how spirited and special his grandmother once was.

But I could feel myself choose not to get sad and sucked through the seaward current of missing you. I instead stayed in that appreciative feeling, thankful for Everett and our moment and our morning, knowing you knew I was thinking of you, knowing you were aware of us.

The choice was simple. I didn't want to sacrifice my energy. It felt too good to be feeling good, and bad thoughts easily bounced off the barrier I had created.

And then I looked down at my walking feet: a Blue Jay feather was sitting on the pavement perfectly intact, so sharp in its sapphire coloring, it honestly looked fake, like it was created for craft store use. The little voice inside my head didn't immediately try to discount the fact that it's only a feather, or rationalize how I could honestly believe it was from you—I just knew it was.

I stood and stared and softly cried looking at that feather, while every answer I've ever had about your death was instantaneously understood—without any worded answers.

The little piece of Blue Jay is now pinned to my vision board, where I'll see it every night before bed, alongside the outlines of another potential property and my goals for this journal. It will be my reminder, not only of you, but to *continually summon my courage and take clear and purposeful action*, for that is one of the meanings of my coveted blue bird.

And speaking of this clear and purposeful action...

In the past few months, I've been editing my entries, re-arranging my proposal, researching potential literary agents, creating and submitting essays for websites to make me "creditable," and writing query letters that meet both individual and particular agency requests.

(And I'm proud to tell you that one of my essays, featured on a popular site called Elephant Journal, received over 2,000 views when it was posted. I couldn't believe it. It felt like confident confirmation that I really can create words worth reading.)

But each time I send material to agents, I just don't completely feel it.

As much as I try to believe that my pitch is going to be read and loved, I more so understand that it's going to get lost in what agents infamously call their "slosh pile," with my words buried beneath thousands of other aspiring authors.

No longer can I wait for an agent to deem me worthy. No longer can I continue polishing my book's proposal, trying to sell myself and the words I began writing after Everett was born.

My written conversations with you have accidentally become about learning to trust and follow the natural flow, as I listen to the signs and my intuition, which continually guide me forward in both the creation of this book and myself. So if these attempts to prove and propose both myself and my work, are no longer where the energy is taking me, I need to bravely follow a new direction.

I've been seeing the numbers 753, showing up not only on the clock, but in amounted totals or addresses, too. They were the same ones I saw while in Maryland, for the Jen Sincero book signing.

Over the course of a few days, the pattern presented itself so many times, I felt compelled to at least search online for the meaning of these numbers, if there even was one.

A woman named JoAnne Walmsley has a book and dedicated web space for the spiritual description of numbers, where I found the following:

The combinations of 7, 5 and 3 mean now is the time to make the necessary changes that will quickly advance you along your life path and your soul mission.

Trust that the angels are supporting, encouraging and guiding you along the way.

This felt like permission to set the proposal aside, trusting that the time and money spent on it, was not wasted. Because I know it got me this far. And now I have to keep running this trail, even though I feel like I'm blindfolded, scared to trip and fall and remain stuck, losing the chance to create these words into all I know they can be.

As for my "soul's mission," as Mrs. Walmsley put it, I know that sounds like a strong description for being published, but this book has always been inside me, and so has the challenge to pursue it. The final product of this book will be my evidence that I am powerful and capable and a creator of my reality. And then I'll be able to merrily continue along my life's path, raising children on that land, in that house—with the unwavering understanding that you are my constant lighted guide.

So I've been researching the self-publishing route, something that I used to think was a cheating way to create a book, but actually, from what I've read, it seems both incredibly modern and smart.

I found an online course all about Amazon publishing, quickly squashing the familiar fear that arises with new opportunity. I didn't hesitate or talk myself out of purchasing it—I simply bought the $97 workshop.

While I educate myself, I trust the next step will be figured out and presented within perfect timing, just as it was when I found the proposal course back in November, right when I needed it. And in the meantime, I'm still editing and proofing and sharpening my journal entries into a story worth reading. Right now, that's my goal for the next few weeks. As well as continuing to grow this lovely little baby.

Grandma told me the other night that she thinks it's a girl. And to me, Grandma is right about everything, especially when it comes to babies.

I haven't allowed myself to admit what I think the gender is, because I was proven entirely wrong with Everett. But I'll follow her hunch, secretly knowing it agrees with mine.

AUGUST 17, 2018

We shall not cease from exploration
And the end of all our exploring
Will be to arrive where we started
And know the place for the first time.

-T.S. Elliot

I'm approaching my 34th week in this pregnancy, which means the baby is the size of a butternut squash, but I can assure you it feels much bigger—every space in my stomach is stretched and filled. Feet and elbows and a little unknown bum, are always poking me, seemingly searching for more room within their confined home.

I have days where I still feel my globe-like belly is bearable, and then other days, I cannot stand having to squat and straddle my legs the way a novice stripper would, as I bend down to pick up toddler toys instead of cash tips.

But as much as I want to stop sharing my body with another human, I'm not entirely ready to share my time with Everett.

How will another child burst through these sewn motherly seams? Because right now, they are sealed shut with only my son, yet it's like I can feel this slow, internal transition: the gentle pulsing of tight strings, beginning to loosen around my heart and create more space.

My recent pattern of thought has been: *How can I love so much again? How can I divide my attention? And when I hold this baby for the first time, am I going to think of Everett? Am I going to miss him in that moment, when I feel my brain immediately embrace his brother or sister?*

I know these questions sound dramatic, but you have to admit, they're valid for a soon-to-be mom of two. I can't be the only woman to have wondered such thoughts.

My favorite thing to eat right now is a turkey sandwich, with mashed avocado, a sprinkle of salt, one fried egg and pea sprouts, swaddled between two pieces of "harvest bread." It's a bakery loaf from Whole Foods that is so deliciously tasty, it causes Chris and I to playfully bicker over who's had more during the week.

That man seems to be more and more in love with my ever-changing body, always telling me how cute or beautiful I look, when he catches me walking through the upstairs naked, with a bowl of cereal cupped in my hands, ready for our side by side movie time together. And for the record, I'm not naked to be scandalous. It's just that by the end of the day, clothes can feel like a hot, tangled layer of tight or unfitting skin, and like a snake, I need to shed them off.

I know Chris is thankful that I'm safely harboring our child. I can tell by the way he gives me space and allows for patience and more privacy, or how he'll now thread his arms under my back and cradle my head with steadying hands, while our bodies come together in the familiar way they know how to.

Each morning, Everett still goes outside and plays, pushing his lawn mower or waving hi to the elder neighbors that walk by. He'll take a few jumps on his little trampoline, then travel over to last summer's wood framed and failed herb garden, which has now been transformed into a sandbox filled with old mismatched measuring cups and trucks.

I make sure to give him a lot of independence, allowing him to do things himself, like picking up his toys before a nap, slipping his shoes on, pulling his pants up, etc. When we comes home from somewhere, he takes off his shoes first thing, and puts them away in the closet. This is honestly a habit his father has yet to consistently remember.

The nesting stage has officially begun.

Just this morning, I decided to put together his two new Ikea bookshelves. It took me over thirty minutes when it would've taken Chris a fraction of time, but I got to sit with Everett and watch him puff with pride when successfully, a bolt he was working with, would finally fall into its fitting place.

The nursery has been emptied of Everett, back to its bare mint colored walls, and the dresser drawers are now slowly being stocked with blankets and onesies and diapers. I have one boy outfit and one girl outfit, washed and folded, waiting to be claimed.

And hundreds of dollars later, after the cost of custom-cut blackout blinds, two gallons of paint (because mama changed her coloring mind), a dresser, and little fixings like the bookshelves, Everett was all ready for the migration over to his "big boy" room. To our surprise, he loves it. I took retired toys from the basement and placed them in a basket, ready for his grand new entrance—it was like a recycled Christmas. When he walked into his room, his face was in a permanent "O," shocked and surprised and excited over the toys, the extra space, and the laid-out train track for his coveted *choo choos.*

At my last prenatal appointment, the midwife asked who would be helping me once the baby came, and immediately I felt a stone drop to the pit of my stomach, crumbling and spreading like the weight of wet sand. I'm supposed to say *my mother.* I'm supposed to say *my mother-in-law.* And even though I remembered this exact question during my first pregnancy, it still felt like the words to my response were stuck in my throat.

Lying, I said my husband would be home for six weeks on paternity leave, and that he would be my main source of help. It's something that his work is currently trying to pass, so while I don't know if it will be cleared before baby time, it was the only thing I could get out.

I could tell the midwife hesitated when typing my answer into her computer chart. I know she wanted to ask, *How about your mother's help?* But whether because my family history form showed your death of breast cancer or something was just sensed, she knew not to ask any further questions. The whole ten second encounter made felt like a defeated, helpless little girl.

It's now been ten years since you died. The 14th of August came and went this year, and while I thought I was going to have a magnificent entry to write to you because of it, I don't.

I can remember after one year passed, trying to imagine what this many would feel like. *Ten years? How will I go ten years with this feeling....with this missing?* But I have. We all have. We've learned to wrestle and wrangle with it, question it, be angry at it, and attempt acceptance, as if we're constantly trying to spread and perfect lumpy icing on a cake that simply won't smooth over quite right.

I'd like to think I've eaten my portioned piece already, like it's since settled into my belly and bones, having become one of the biggest ratios of myself. That's why on the night that marked you leaving this physical place, I simply crawled into bed extra early and alone, but not because I was sad—I was just ready to be done with the background distraction of *ten years ten years*, and for the relief of tomorrow to come.

As I fell asleep, I thought about lying in bed with you at home, during those last minutes of your life. I thought about the things Dad said, as Allison and I witnessed what seemed like two separate parts of you, struggling to figure out which way to continue. One wanted to keep you physically here. And the other was slowly stealing your breath, pulling you closer and closer into the "impalpable" energy you now inhabit.

He kept telling you it was okay to let go. *Let go, Jen. It's okay. We're going to be okay. The kids will be alright. Just let go sweetheart.* He continually gave you the permission you silently needed.

While I can't explain what it was like to watch you literally leave your body, I can say I envy the way you were guided onward by Dad. I'll never forget it for the rest of my life.

I was there when you took your last breath out of this world, and you were there when I took my first one into it. Now as I sit here, saying all of this to you, I'm thinking forward to the moment this baby takes his or her first breath of air. For the only thing that truly separates you and I, I'm still able to take into my lungs, while you simply cannot.

I can't see this essential air. I can't taste it. I can't touch it. But it's a gas that is all around, one that everything—the plants and animals and humans, need to survive.

And just like this invisible air, I know you're still all around me. And just like I couldn't live without it, I know I couldn't live without you, even after all these years. From my first breath, to your last breath, to now—I've never known a life without you.

I'll never have to.

SEPTEMBER 28, 2018

thirty months + thirty-nine weeks

How you deal with your energy flow has a major effect on your life. If you assert your will against the energy of an event that has already happened, it is like trying to stop the ripples caused by a leaf dropped into a still lake. Anything you do causes more disturbance, not less. When you resist, the energy has no place to go. It gets stuck in your psyche and seriously affects you. It blocks your heart's energy flow and causes you to feel closed and less vibrant. This is literally what is happening when something is weighing on your mind or when things just get too heavy for you. This is the human predicament.

-Michael Singer, *The Untethered Soul*

For the past three weeks, I've written and edited and deleted several entries to you, all of which were about this baby and how I'm feeling for the soon-to-be delivery.

I eventually gave up my efforts, knowing words worthy of this journal were simply not going to come out before the baby does; my "flow" or whatever you want to call it, had simply stopped, and each entry I typed to you, lacked everything I treasure these entries for having: connection and love and the feeling of real conversation with my spirit of a mother.

But while Everett and I were playing out on the porch this morning, so many Blue Jays began flying around and within my yard's two adjacent oak trees, that it was honestly alarming. The birds seemed to be in an argument amongst one another, at such high volume, it felt my attention was being personally sought out.

So I gave some silent acknowledgement: *Okay. I'll write the final "pre-baby" entry today. I get the message...*

Somehow it felt like you who was out there calling, asserting to stop this resistance against writing, and just finish it already. Because once this baby is born, the opportunity for a September entry will have entirely passed.

All I presently think about is labor and *when.*

It's like I'm standing within a backroad's blind spot, waiting for a semi-truck to travel around the bend and topple me with surprise, pain, and incredible amounts of joy and love.

Dramatic, but it's how I feel, less than a week from my due date.

Chris and I went out to dinner date the other night, a little farewell to life as we know it, as we sat and talked about how much we love Everett and how funny he is and how ready we are for this second baby to come.

He thinks it's a girl.

I told him "her" name can be translated to "lady of the sea," and he laughed, because he knows my quirky love for mermaids, even telling me often that I look like one, the way my hair naturally rests above the small of my back.

Before our meal was served, I went to the bathroom. Once I emptied my bladder for the twentieth time that day, while washing my hands, I paused and took in the familiar shape of my belly's reflection, knowing the next time I'd be at this favorite restaurant we like to frequent, I'll have met our named baby.

When I turned, there on the wall was a huge mural of a mermaid, looking sexy and beautiful in her painted skin as I stared back at her, wondering what all is soon to come around that blinding bend.

Like this symbolic last supper, I've been checking off lists and completing little rituals of organizing and going to Target twice a week for who knows what at this point, as a way of feeling prepared for what I simply cannot prepare for.

My laundry has been washed and folded more often than usual, because ideally, I'd like an empty hamper when I leave for the hospital. I go into the nursery where majority of my things are packed, just to stand there and basically stare, rearranging the way my coconut water and snack bars are positioned on the dresser, as if I'm playing a game of Tetris, trying to get things to look and fit right, in a pointless attempt of mentally inducing labor.

My kitchen cabinets have been wiped down. The closets have been organized so that our clothes can properly welcome the changing season. Everett's favorite foods have been stocked numerous times, and I've trimmed his nails over and over (which has to be done with the bribery of M&M's), prepping him as if I'm going to be gone for two months instead of two nights.

No longer will I be only his mother. No longer will I be a mother of one—the mother I've loved getting to know and grow into over the past two and some years. Yes I'll still be *me*, but there's no denying my person is going to shift and rearrange once again. Perhaps that's why I have this odd idea of disappearing into thin air and away from my son.

While I know I can have things done and gathered and cleaned, no matter how many times I vacuum my living room carpet, it won't change the natural timing of this birth. As I learned with Everett, the "when" is out of my hands.

If I don't go into labor by October 5th, which is three days after my due date, I'll be induced to avoid having another large baby, which apparently accompanies a higher risk of shoulder dystocia.

I have really been trying to separate my experience delivering Everett, from whatever is going to happen with this delivery. Over and over, I'd catch myself remembering his birth as if it had just happened, and therefore mentally prepare for another twenty-six hour labor, that damn shoulder dystocia, the hospital transfer, no recovery time, and qualms with breastfeeding.

So to help me reverse this harmful thinking, I've written in my pen and paper journal daily, affirming that this time, things will be different—that they may not be perfect or easy or even drug-free, but they are going to be different.

I love thinking of Chris holding another baby.

The nurses and midwife on-call will all be perfect for me and baby.

It will be good to have Allison in the delivery room.

I have new pajamas waiting for me.

The baby's name will suit them.

Everett will be happy at home.

Every time I use affirmations—whether writing or thinking them...whether about labor or simply loving myself—I immediately feel better. I can actually feel my energy lift as that upward shift happens, remembering I'm in control of how I feel, always and without exception.

On our daily walk this morning, as I pushed the stroller and controlled Clifford on the leash, I was telling myself things like:

Labor is going to be much faster than with Everett.

You won't pop blood vessels in your eyes and face because of an infant's stuck shoulder—this baby is going to slide right out, just as it should.

(I'd say it's a good thing my passing walking neighbors can't hear my thoughts.)

But I was truly trying to visualize this baby being delivered by a few strong pushes, with no hindrances, and exiting my body in the "easy" way it's meant to.

After we got back, I wanted to water the fall-colored burgundy mums I bought for my front porch (apparently I'm even trying to prep my plants for my laboring absence), so I freshly filled my watering can with kitchen sink water, while Everett was playing with the bunny cage, trying to wedge one of his toy cars between the metal bars.

No matter how many times I tell him to *not touch the bunny*, he simply cannot leave that poor rabbit alone. It's the same with my new flowers. He picks the buds off and tosses them into unknown places.

Anyways, when I started watering, the long and narrow tipped-over spout wouldn't release anything, as if the container was entirely empty and I hadn't just replenished it.

Seriously confused, I kept tipping, until the can was almost upside down and then *bam!*

A mum bud, big enough to entirely clog the spout, popped out with such pressuring force, water exploded in a steady and outward stream.

It literally looked like a baby had *slid right out*, just as I'd been trying to imagine happening within my body, moments before.

I couldn't stop laughing, and began feeling that familiar warmth of assurance coursing through me, knowing my attempts to think positive were not falling onto deaf ears—that somehow, I am indeed being heard.

So this is my official surrender.

I am ready. I am open. I am even done cleaning.

I'm so close to becoming a mother of two...so ready to hold this baby and know who they are.

Mom, please be with me.

NOVEMBER 4, 2018

thirty-two months + one month old

yours is the light by which my spirit's born:
yours is the darkness of my soul's return
you are my sun, my moon, and all my stars

(- e.e cummings)

On October 5th, we welcomed our little lady of the sea, Marion Maine.

She is healthy and beautiful and exactly who I gently imagined bringing into this world throughout the entire pregnancy. For all that time, I hoped my girl was making her way to me—and she was.

It feels as if I somehow dreamed this sweet, petite petunia into my life.

On induction morning, I got up at 4:30 a.m. and showered, had coffee with Chris, placed hot rollers in my hair, and did my makeup as the curlers set. Nana and Allison came to the house, and together, they got Everett up and fed him the breakfast he refuses to stray from: vanilla greek yogurt from Trader Joe's.

Chris got our hospital bags and pillows and the down comforter I insisted on bringing, packed into the car. He dusted off the finishing small details, like showing Nana how to work the TV remote and reading through the lengthy "Everett directions" I wrote, making sure she knew his routine. This was all Chris' way of carrying some of my nerves, and I appreciated that we were a team, even though it was me who had the job of physically delivering a baby in the next coming hours.

In the car, I stayed quiet. Chris had NPR on and I listened to one of my meditation tapes through silencing earphones. A few minutes into it, Esther Hicks said this:

You can't overcome hardship or stand stubbornly within it. You've got to reach the place where you accept it's easy...and then it will be easy. And when people ask, "How was it easy?" You say:

I made it a struggle a lot longer than I needed to. It was easy because the energy was already there and the momentum had been gathered and things were already aligned. I just had to do one piece: I just had to relax a little and trust a little and try a little less hard. I just had to stop justifying and rationalizing and defending. I had to feel worthy without the needs for justification.

And hearing that little part, felt as if her words were coming through my ears and into my heart, preparing me for what was ahead.

I accepted that this birth was going to be easy. I knew I didn't have to *stand stubbornly within hardship*...that I didn't have to be headstrong and refuse an epidural if I wanted one. I knew any choice I made in the delivery room, didn't need justification.

I trusted that everything I thought and journaled and affirmed about this birth in the months and weeks prior, did indeed shift this whole soon-to-be event into right alignment.

Before entering the hospital's parking garage, we made a right turn onto "Marion Street." It confirmed that the old-fashioned girl name I had on reserve, was the right choice. Just like the street sign, over the past year, I have seen her name in varying and random ways, as if something else had chosen what to call her, long before she was mine.

Perhaps she always knew who she was. Perhaps she always knew she'd be my child.

We checked in at the maternity ward and were shown to our room. It was spacious and settled within a corner, with two glass windows, allowing a view of the current sunrise. It was comforting and secluded and I was grateful to feel like things were continually going right.

The midwife on-call checked in with me, explaining how the induction would work. Before Pitocin, she was going to put a Foley bulb into my cervix, which basically just creates pressure and promotes dilation. It looked like a strange flexible balloon, with a bubble at the top and three sets of tubing attached and hanging.

She inserted the bulb part and with a syringe, slowly pushed a saline solution through the tubing, therefore expanding the bulb and hopefully my cervix.

Once it was secured into place, all I felt were period-like cramps, and I was still able to walk around the room and use the bathroom. I just had three tubes hanging out of me, peeking through my open-back hospital gown. Chris and Allison got a kick out of that one.

For two or so hours, this bulb sat in me. Finally, it fell out on its own (which is ideal—that means it did its expanding job) and I said aloud that I thought my water broke. It felt like slow trickles were puddling on the bed underneath me.

This early sign of labor made me giddy and confident, like another check had been marked off under the criteria of easy. I truly just kept energetically floating down river and now as I'm reflecting, I can honestly say there's never been a time in my life when I was that *in the flow.*

There really is such power in trust and surrender.

Pitocin started to drip into my plotted vein and contractions began soon after, each one coming about every one to two minutes, which is ridiculously close together when compared to starting labor naturally.

During a contraction break, all three of us would talk, and then without warning, I'd close my eyes and get quiet and nod off into the tightening sensations within my belly. I remember Chris once saying to me, "See ya later!" in the funny Everett voice we like to mimic, because I'd truly disappear into myself as I concentrated on each contraction, knowing the pain was pulling our baby further and further down into me.

When I began to feel sweaty and frequently became more silent, I wanted my dilation checked. Knowing what was ahead, I questioned if I wanted to continue onward without an epidural. I was remembering Everett's birth, picturing the room where I labored, the things I said and felt and thought, like I was being pulled back into that memory. And I wanted nothing to do with it.

Prior to this second labor, I thought I had to be brave and choose a drug-free birth again, so I could...I don't, *face it.* But I quickly recognized that reasoning equaled a wall of resistance; a rift in the feel-good river I was riding.

So without justifying and rationalizing and defending—without wanting to once again fight and prove how strong I could be, I simply looked up at my midwife and said in clear words, "I want the epidural," even though I had just been checked at 6cm and labor was proving to progress quickly.

She said, "Are you sure?" And without letting her slight and silent disagreement hinder my decision, I repeated a short and confident *yes,* looking directly in her eyes, politely portraying the message that I knew what I wanted.

The surrender was simple and accepted and felt right. I was proud of myself.

Getting the actual epidural was easy, and my anesthesiologist was one of the most serious, calm, confident, and well-carried men I've ever encountered. He was the kind of man you would've found attractive, almost as if you had personally sought him out to be my doctor. I can't explain it—that's just the feeling I had as soon as he walked into my room, like you were pushing me forward within my choice of drugs, delivering them to me on a good-looking platter of encouragement.

When I felt the relief from contractions, that epidural became the most liberating piece of permission I ever gave myself. Instead of reaching the point of screaming and panic and digging into the deepest parts of me just to remain breathing, I laid in bed watching the Kardashians, with my sister and husband...my two best friends.

Within forty-five minutes, my dilation was casually checked, and the midwife said, "Oh! You could start pushing if you want."

I was so shocked and excited and in disbelief at how incredibly different the entire experience was narrating.

Chris and Allison got on either side of me and held up my legs; they were just numb enough that lifting them took more effort than normal. And in the lower left side of my abdomen, I could still feel when I was getting a contraction, but the sensation was mild, peaking through so I knew when it was time to push. To me, this all meant that I had been given a fabulous epidural—not too much, not too little.

Pushing was fun. With my hair done and makeup on, as shallow as it may sound, I felt not only strong, but beautiful. I felt like me. I was clear and focused and only had one job to do: push the baby out. And the room was calm. Only my nurse and midwife were there, who helped as she casually sat on the edge of the bed and nonchalantly cheered me on with encouragement.

Allison and Chris did, too, and when I'd hear their voices grow in excitement, I knew I was getting closer and closer.

Within ten minutes, the final push came and Marion truly did slide right out, just like that mum bud.

I looked up at Allison; she had tears glazed in her eyes and an awe-frozen face as she was seeing the baby lay between my legs. For a passing second, I felt you. Your girls were together, experiencing one of the most beautiful moments this life can offer.

When people say things to me like, "Oh your Mom would be so proud!" it sounds like you are missing—that if only you were still living, you'd get the chance to acknowledge my accomplishments. But it's within the moments like the one above, that my body pulses with that pride, and I'm utterly aware of you—of that fact that it's not *would be* proud but *is*.

They laid Marion on my chest but her legs were folded closed. I kept saying, "What is it? What is it!" anxiously awaiting the most anticipated information of the past nine months.

"It's a boy!" Chris looked at me and said with this huge smile I can still vividly remember. But my stomach sank because something just didn't completely feel right.

He tried again. "It's a girl!" And everyone, including myself, laughed, as I laid my head back on the pillow and cried with the relief that she was out, she was healthy, and she really was a girl. I had done it.

Her birth was truly one of the best days of my life. From start to finish, everything worked out. Never have I manifested something so accurate and with such knowing ease, receiving so many assuring signs in the weeks leading up to her delivery. She feels like the ultimate proof of all I've written about in this journal.

Marion is the very piece that revolved me entirely from Everett's birth, and all I have become since. I feel as if I've now spun into my very own rotation, under my own guiding light. And because of her, I know my power.

I promise I'll write again soon, when everyone's needs (including mine) have been met, and I have a few moments to talk with you.

Now that Marion is here...now that I've truly settled into the most comfortable and confident places within myself and motherhood because of her birth, I'm already feeling like I need you less and less, which is both a hardening yet honest thought.

DECEMBER 1, 2018

thirty-three months + two months

Over rivers and valleys, mountains and plains
Over all you have lost and all you have gained
Over all you have gathered and all you let go
You have traveled at length through the wild unknowns
And through all that is changing you can see you have
grown
You have walked in the light, you have not been alone

-Morgan Harper Nicholas

Marion has managed to blend into our family with such ease, it's hard remembering life without a daughter—that not so long ago, she was still just a star, waiting to be brought home to us.

Each day gets a little better; Chris and I get more sleep, my routine takes a sharper shape, and I understand Marion's needs better.

Everett has adjusted well to having a sister. I'll catch him giving her kisses when she's in her swing, or he will run over and gently plug her mouth with a binky if she's crying. And on our beloved Trader Joe's trips, he still says hi to everyone, but now makes sure to also introduce his new friend, as he points to Marion and repeats, "Baby, baby, baby!"

I'm the one who had a strange time adjusting to two.

When I got home from the hospital, my first priority was to put Everett down for bed. With so much about to change, I needed him to know that our routine was going to stay the same.

Sore, tired, and bleeding into an adult diaper, I gently crawled into his big boy bed and laid beside him, just as I always had before. All I could do was cry though, because suddenly, it felt so different, like I was having a strange and silent affair within my heart for Marion. He was no longer my only baby, and the sudden transition made me feel scared, dropped in a place I'd never been before.

Seeing me cry, despite the efforts I tried to hinder my tears, Everett took his blanket and willingly wiped my eyes. His ability for compassion and the soft sweetness that comprises his personality entirely, makes me so incredibly proud he's mine: in one of my most vulnerable moments as a mother, my son held me and just that *feeling* of him, assured me everything would eventually be okay and I'd adjust appropriately in time.

As Grandma has joked before, you don't grow an extra set of hands when you have another baby. And as I've realized, nor do you grow another brain or heart—you just simply make more room, dividing up the attention and love.

And I haven't forgotten to keep some space for myself.

Learning how to be selfish was a milestone within my motherhood.

When my needs are met, I'm able to take better care of my babies— when I'm replenished and full, I am capable of watering my flowers and guiding their growth, all while remaining in love with myself, knowing I need nourishment, too.

It seems simple enough, but with Everett, why was it so hard to make it to the shower? Why was it so hard to leave the house alone and without guilt?

Because I started off motherhood thinking that sacrifice was what I was supposed to do—that sacrifice meant I loved Everett most. But I don't want my kids (however many I end up having) to represent what I gave up for them. They will be my life's work, there's no doubt about that, but I will not lose myself in the process.

Jessie got married two weeks ago in Maryland. It was the event I've been anticipating since January, and the day truly unfolded with perfection for my most deserving friend.

Everett was left at home with Allison; we only brought the baby, and treated the weekend as a short getaway from our toddler and the routines of home.

For the entire wedding night, I wore Marion in the Moby wrap, which sadly covered from my waist up, the beautiful Anthropologie jumpsuit I treated myself to for the big day. But she slept like a pouched kangaroo and never cried. The only sound she made was a little burp when Jessie and Justin were exchanging their vows.

Seeing your best friend marry the right man is a wonderful feeling. I can now know and trust that the things she dreams of, are secure for her taking, like babies. She will most likely be my first best friend to turn mom friend, something that literally thrills me.

And while my daughter was wrapped to me on the dance floor, with a drink in one hand, and a stand-by binky in the other, I felt alive and accomplished and an accumulated version of the mother I have always wanted to be.

I felt like you, all blended into me.

People would come up and gently shout over the music and into my ear, "I want to be a mom like you when I have kids!" And something within me pridefully swelled with each drunken comment, as if I was somehow an example to my friends and the friends of strangers, that you can still keep yourself when you have a child.

When I first found out I was pregnant, I envisioned myself with red lipstick, drinking a beer, and breastfeeding my baby at this beautiful wedding. But my lips were still bare, my beer had a straw (that's how it's most comfortable to drink), and my boobs were dried up, for reasons that unlike with Everett, I'm not going to explain over three or so spanning entries.

Minutes before we arrived at Jessie's venue, out in the middle of farmlands, I happened to look up and out the car window with in-sync timing, seeing one of those marquee lettered church signs that read:

Strive for progress, not perfection.

And I quickly knew to kick the whiner inside my head that was poo-pooing because my lips still weren't brightly colored with lipstick, even after all this time. Because I have indeed made incredible progress, when back in July, I found a doctor who prescribed a medicine I take once a week, and each month, my lips seem to get a little better.

Even though I am still within my healing process, I know without a doubt, I would've never gotten this far in my beliefs or personal growth, had it not been for this condition, which forced me to keep believing, keep appreciating, keep meditating, keep trusting.

Source always gives you what you need, in order to get you where you want to go. I guess that's why *be careful for what you wish for* is a line everyone knows.

At my six-week check-up, there were several other new mothers in the waiting room, all of which had their own moms with them for help and those extra set of hands. I was obviously the only one alone.

For Everett's first appointment, I would've cried seeing those other mothers, thinking that I was permanently crippled and incapable because I wouldn't have your help or guidance or support. But this time around, I felt like a straight boss, simply because I chose to.

During my exam, Everett was occupied in his stroller, eating a packed mini pizza, and I had Marion in the Moby (surprise), while I laid on my back and got my vagina checked and cleared. The whole scenario caught me affirming in my mind over and over: *I am an awesome mother.*

Because it's not a bad thing to love yourself. And constantly reminding our minds to tell us good things is our strongest super power.

The way we speak to ourselves matters—it's just a point of making positive talk a habit and having the audacity to believe the things you tell yourself. For so long, I was scared to mentally affirm I was beautiful because what if I really wasn't? What if no one else believed I was? But that truth is up to no one but me. And whether or not I believe I'm a good mom is up to no one but me.

I wrote a pretend check last year for a certain amount of money, printing "FALL 2018" on its front, and on the signature line, "for house and property." I playfully imagined the cash coming from a book deal.

When Chris and I began looking at land this past summer, I started seeing see 2:17 on the clock, on a regular basis. I couldn't understand what it meant for weeks, until I realized that the check's referencing number was 217. So from then on, I truly believed this money was coming one way or another. I truly believed the land was coming, just not in the way that it all recently came to be.

A few months before Marion was born, we found another wooded lot for sale. It's almost five acres and it's on top of a hill, two criteria that met my desires with perfection. Each time we visited the land, I could picture where our house would be. I pictured Clifford prancing free in his Wheaton-breed ways, and how I'd call the kids in for dinner after they'd been playing outside and under the trees.

In my journal, there are property descriptions and child-like drawings of our future driveway and views, which now seem to have been magically traced from that space of pen and paper, onto this framed piece of land. There's even a little creek that runs along the bottom—a total bonus. And within the past years, I would tease Chris, telling him I was going to have a trail around our house, so that I could walk out my door and into the woods, with a stroller and the dog.

Well wouldn't ya know, there is a nature reserve surrounding our dotted property lines, just like the previous lot we loved, with an already established walking path. While it's currently overgrown and rugged, it's a start to that once imaginary trail.

The Universe delivered. And it's not just because I'm lucky or one of those annoying people who have everything handed to them: it's simply because I got specific and intentional, and chose to believe that there was a power working things out for me.

When we first started flirting with the idea of buying land, we figured out all the ways to scrape together our current home's equity, our savings, and another loan. But now we are in the financial position to actually do this—both the land and the house, because Chris got a new job.

(I feel like I am telling you too many new things at once, but a lot has happened since Marion's birth.)

He secured an interview in New York City for Amazon Web Services. I was surprised he had searched for change, because we've been comfortable financially and he loves his current job at Carnegie Mellon.

But for two weeks, he was absent from himself, preparing for the infamously challenging interview, and I knew I just had to pull up my big girl pants and leave him be, allowing Chris to do what he does when he knows there's a job to be done.

One day after the interview, he was offered a position, and because of his constant drive to move forward with his work and the ability to provide, that vision check is real. Our land is real. Our house is real.

The property will be ready to purchase in spring 2019. And our current elder neighbor used to build houses for a living, so when I ran into him the other day while on a quick walk without the kids, I told him our plans, and he recommended an architect. It felt like another stepping pebble was simply handed to me, like the Universe was saying, "Here sweetheart! Keep up the positivity and appreciation!"

Literally, everything is coming together, just as I tried so hard to believe throughout these conversations with you.

All that's left, is this book. Which perhaps coincidentally, I've definitely decided to publish through Amazon.

When the time comes for its launch, I fear it will get lost in a sea of online novels, or that no one is going to want to read a stranger's journal. *What if no one relates to anything I've written? What if everyone thinks I'm crazy because I think my mother sends me Blue Jay feathers? What will Grandma think when she finds out I have a vision board dream of smoking topless on my back porch?*

It's all really scary. But that's how I know it's right and ready and ripe for the taking. I must believe that the Universe or God or Source, will take care of the details and allow this work to become all I know it can be.

In the foreseeable future, I know I need to figure out how to format these entries from a Microsoft Word document, into book pages. And I need an illustrator for the cover. And I need to start creating an e-mail list to send out digital copies of the book before it launches on Amazon, for the purpose of reviews—without them, a self-published book will plummet. I learned all of this from that $97 course I purchased, which I'm obviously very thankful I found.

It would be pretty surreal to have this book real and physical and ready to buy by Mother's Day—that particular timing just feels fitting.

I am scared to write this, but I think this is the last entry, Mom. Even though putting a stop to our talks feels like another form of goodbye, it suddenly seems natural and right to allow our ending.

Everything just feels complete, a realization that came the moment Chris corrected himself in the delivery room and said Marion was a girl, like she was my very own physical evidence of something I still don't fully understand.

Now that I have a daughter, I can only hope she will one day love me as much as I love you. That when I travel onward, she will think of me as often as I think of you, and she'll carry within and throughout her, every ounce of my spirit, as she constantly holds me both in her mind and heart.

Because that is what I do with you.

And I hope to teach her, through my example, how to be her own mothering sun—how to nourish both herself in her own becomings, as well as her kindred flowers.

Because that is what you did for me.

PART FOUR
1 ENTRY

APRIL 23, 2019

three years + six months

It's dark because you are trying too hard. Lightly child, lightly. Learn to do everything lightly. Yes, feel lightly even though you're feeling deeply. Just lightly let things happen and lightly cope with them. I was so serious in those days... throw away your baggage and go forward. There are quicksands all about you, sucking at your feet, trying to suck you down into fear and self-pity and despair. That is why you must walk so lightly. Lightly my darling...

-Aldous Huxley, *Island*

Well, here I am again—I've waited since we last talked in December to write this entry.

Aside from this current conversation, the book is now completed—it's been bound and printed and proofed into pages of an actual paperback book; my nightstand has been decorated with practice copies I'd ordered from Amazon, round after round, trying to perfect each paragraph and front cover hue.

The creation process has been challenging, but for some reason, the details all seem unnecessary to write out.

Because I got *here.* I got to the last and final chapter of this journal, with everything before it now completed. And that's what matters. This is where I want to start the end.

I went to an Abraham Hicks workshop last weekend in Asheville, North Carolina. And am still trying to understand everything I felt and heard—it changed my life, for reasons I cannot pin down quite yet.

A lot had to happen in order for me to get there. I spent $500 on my workshop ticket. And then came booking the flight, and according plans with Jessie, who was luckily willing to meet me there, in the town where she and her husband had honeymooned back in November. And I was gone from my family over Easter weekend, leaving both kids with Chris for the first time.

While I got to function freely for a weekend without children, as soon as I parked at the Pittsburgh airport, it didn't feel right to be without them...like my limbs had become numb without the familiar weight of baby Marion.

The last time you and I talked, I didn't know this wonderful news— but, Jessie is pregnant, almost half way along. So she'll indeed be my "first friend turned mom friend."

Once she picked me up from the Asheville airport, we checked into our Marriott, and when she and I were settled in bed, chatting the way best friends do, I felt the baby kick my hand. I will remember it always. She cried with relief, able to accept that the movements she'd been feeling weren't gas or mindless belly happenings—that indeed, her baby was real and well and thriving.

Early the next morning, she took a yoga class and went to brunch and explored her favorite little city, after dropping me off at the Omni Grove Park Inn, a resort-type setting where the workshop was to be held.

Its entrance was rustic, but in a luxurious way, with velvet couches and over-sized rocking chairs placed around a big roaring fire. Mountains and blooming trees were outside of every surrounding window.

For a moment, I stood in this entry, turning my body in each compassing direction, not knowing where to go. But someone asked if I was there for the Abraham event...I said yes, and followed them.

At the check-in desk, I proudly showed my previously printed and signed registration form, got a sticky name tag, and walked into the conference room, with about 400 chairs to choose seating from. I ended up sitting next to a Canadian gentleman in his mid-fifties (that's a guess). He was friendly and bubbly and so genuinely excited to be there, it made me feel like I'd found a destined pal for the day.

When Ester walked in (remember, she channels a spirit called Abraham, but Esther is her real name), there was music playing and everyone stood up and cheered and I felt elated. This woman, whose voice and printed words I've read and listened and wrote to you about for over two years now—there she was.

After a quick introduction, she got quiet for a few moments, taking long slow breaths in, getting herself clear and connected. And then the workshop started.

There was what's called a "hot seat" on stage, with a microphone and bright lights to make it all look terrifying. People would be chosen, come to the seat, ask a question, and then from there, a discussion was brought forth.

I had pit stains down to my waist when I knew it was time to raise our hands; because out of the four or so chances that came to get into the infamous chair, I struck mine into the air.

After each hour of discussion, there was a twenty-minute break in between, and I'd leave the room for a moment, feeling like I didn't know what to do with what I'd just heard. It was overwhelming, because I finally realized that *this shit is real.*

Just seeing and hearing Esther talk, made every doubt I had about energy diminish entirely, and answered my planned question of: *How do I know my mother is still here? How do I feel like I'm not fooling myself when I choose to believe in her?*

I just feel like I have failed you because I truly thought I was going to write this last entry, saying that my lips have entirely healed— it's the very last thing to yet manifest on my vision board. I wanted to tell you that I believed enough these past few months, and then BAM!...end this book with a sense of perfection.

I'm embarrassed to even still be writing about my lips, because I don't want people to think, *Is this girl serious? Why is she making such a big deal about them?*

But I'm not a pansy. And I never wanted to dilute our conversations the way my pen and paper journals are, with worrying and attempted affirmations and details of doctor visits. So I know I haven't properly portrayed the impact this "illness" has had in my life since it started two spring seasons ago.

It has continually made me feel like my ankles are stuck in the mud, even though my entire body is now in the light: we have our house plans drawn out...I got my baby girl...I created this book, and our property is waiting to be put in our name within the next month.

And even though I have all these beautiful things, I seem to be stationed, staring at my feet—which is why I *still*, even after all that's happened and come to be, have a difficult time believing that I create my reality. Because surely if that were true, I'd be free by now.

This all makes me think of an Esther (Abraham) Hicks recording I once heard, from a workshop that took place back in 1990. (Yes, these workshops have been going on for a long time.)

It played through my headphones on YouTube one morning, while I twirled my hair into hot rollers during Everett's nap, and Esther said something like this:

I want you to imagine a magical city...a beautiful city that was small, but perfect. There are beautiful interests everywhere, so to live and be in this city is a wonderful experience. Even the arteries of traffic run smoothly. Except there's a pothole on sixth avenue. And instead of focusing on all the positive aspects this city has to offer, humans are so consumed with the negative effects of things, that all anyone is focused on is the pothole.

And then she continued with another example, which made me freeze the fiddling fingers within my hair, and put my hands around the bathroom sink for physical support, as I slowly shook my head from side to side and silently cried...

Let's picture a young woman whose been deemed terminally ill by her doctor. And yet majority of her body is still as this magic city; it is well, and the arteries of traffic continue to run smoothly. But because of the attention the doctor has given, she's placing all of her focus on the pothole, until it eventually consumes her city.

It felt like she was somehow talking about you.

So it seems I must live out an intentional life—not only for myself, but for you. Because no longer can you consciously choose to focus on that beautiful city; but I can. And I must trust the potholes were directly put on my path by an all-knowing power, who knows what it's doing. I'd rather accept this Universal magic into my life, rather than waking up each day angry or mad or confused at why certain things are the way there are, and instead, *look for the good.*

Anyways. On Sunday, the second workshop day, I walked into the conference room at the same time as my Canadian friend, who already had a seat saved. I was thankful for the coincidence.

The first person to sit in the hot seat, stated that his mother had just died Friday, and every ounce of my attention became concentrated.

I felt like everything Esther was saying relative to the non-physical world, I had already read and learned and finally, at that moment, gave myself permission to fully believe.

Because in front of me, I saw this forty-seven-year-old man, cry, trying to understand this question of death—even though the very first person he met at this event was named Louise, his late mother's name.

It took me too many years to understand the ways non-physical chooses to communicate with us. And I think for a while, I didn't want to believe what I knew, because I still wanted to think that you really were just gone—in some ways, that scenario is easier. There's no believing, no meditating, no effort to be different than the sad-sayers I seem to encounter within every social situation.

Because if I vibrate low, you really do disappear.

At the end of the hour session, I went up to this man. He was tall and good looking and I felt like a baby ant standing under him. But I grabbed both of his forearms and blurted out with choked back tears melting into my mascara, "I was seventeen when I lost my mother...when she *transitioned*....and it took me ten years to finally find her. But I did. And you will find your mom too—you did as soon as you walked into this room and found the woman named Louise. I know it seems silly for someone younger to be telling you these things, but trust me. This will all make sense someday."

He had tears in his eyes and was nodding his head, and I knew he understood what I meant. His question was supposed to be asked, not mine. Because apparently, I had already known my answer.

Seeing his face and remembering what it felt like to initially lose you, made me walk out of there and call Jessie to have her come get me, even though there were still two hours left. I didn't want to stay, because I had gotten what I came for, which was the reassurance that I've been driving down the right road to finding you...

But I haven't been fooling myself. I've been becoming myself.

When I walked out of the Omni and towards Jessie's Jeep, the spring breeze hit my face, and I exploded in tears, swiftly picking up my pace to get to the privacy of her passenger seat.

And as soon as I sat, it all just settled into my bones. Everything. The past ten years was swallowed with a big gulp, and I realized these conversations had finally found their ending. It all simply felt over, like *what else do you need to do Hayley? What else do you need to read or hear or travel to in order to just understand what your heart already does?*

I immediately felt silly for leaving my family. I felt guilty being away from my children. But I also felt elated that the answers I came down to Asheville looking for, were already written in this journal.

It was all a moment of absolutely clarity, even though I literally couldn't see because my eyes were so glossed with tears.

And while leaving the hotel, I was riding down the elevator, thinking of how happy I was to be returning to Chris and my babies. Held in my hands, I looked at the printed check-out confirmation, and in big, bold letters the Marriott's goodbye message was:

You are ready to move forward.

I smiled and I knew.

So it's done. It is all done. I thought it was the moment Marion was born. Or I thought it would be when I was completely healed. But not until this trip, was I entirely ready to move forward from this journaled journey. Now I can allow these words to fall into the right hands of the right readers, with the perfect May timing I had hoped for.

I have gotten to where I intended to go, and even though I will always have confusing paths to travel, I've arrived at wherever this place of refusing to doubt you (and myself) ever again resides.

And on the way to getting here, I got to tell your story, while actively creating mine.

I do not think seventy years is the time of a man or woman

Nor that seventy million years is the time of a man or woman

Nor that years will ever stop the existence of me or anyone else.

Is it wonderful that I should be immortal? as everyone is immortal,

I know it is wonderful...but my eyesight is equally wonderful ...and how I was conceived in my mother's womb is equally wonderful.

And that my soul embraces you this hour, and we affect each other without ever seeing each other, is every bit as wonderful:

And that I think such thoughts as these is just as wonderful, And that I can remind you, and you think them and know them to be true is just as wonderful.

And that the moon spins round the earth and on with the earth is equally wonderful,

And that they balance themselves with the **sun** and stars is equally wonderful.

-Walt Whitman, Leaves of Grass [Who Learns My Lesson Complete]

acknowledgements:

I would like to thank each person who read the little blog I kept and posted to social media for nearly three years—each encouraging comment kept me within the belief that this journal could become something. And a lot of you became members of my "Book Launch Team," which helped with the initial upload to Amazon. Without your reviews, this book's success wouldn't have been possible.

Thank you to Samira, who illustrated this beautiful cover and inside illustrations, from her home in Germany, and who exchanged over one hundred e-mails with me. You captured the feeling of this book completely, and I am so thankful for the connection we made.

To my husband, Chris—you are my very best friend. And I know that's the foundation of our happiness (and early bedtimes for the kids). Thank you for holding the strings to my ninety-nine red balloons, keeping me grounded within your reality, as I dream up the details of our life together.
And to his beautiful sister Lauren, thank you for all your help re-sizing the cover and working your magic in Adobe photoshop.

I owe this entire journal to my Nana—she's the one who encouraged me to keep a diary when I was just a young girl.
I love you a million bushels. You are my special piece of Mom.

My siblings are the best gift my mother ever gave me: Allison, Cole and Tatum—I love you, and together, we are the only humans on this entire planet that are physically comprised of Mom.
May you live each day knowing she is living on within you.

And thank you to all the mothers who have helped me become my own: Aunt Sara, Grandma, Judy, Terri, and my "Mrs. Treml."

And to Jessie, Kati and Meghan....my best friends who have cheered me on throughout this entire project. And Steph, you're my lifelong friend.

My mother (36) with my youngest sister, Tatum.

ABOUT THE AUTHOR:

Hayley is twenty-nine years old, married to her best friend and mother of two children. Returning to their roots, she and her husband recently moved to the small town outside of Pittsburgh where they both grew up, and built a house on acres of wooded land, tucked away on a rural hillside. She imagines expanding their family as the little homestead grows.

She has taught yoga for the past ten years and is now a newly certified birth doula. Self-care and babies/children are her passionate teachings.

Mother Sun is her first novel.

To follow more journal writings, visit *hayleypearlman.com*

*If you enjoyed this book, please leave an Amazon review!